I GREW UP LITTLE

Finding Hope in a Big God

Patsy Clairmont

W PUBLISHING GROUP™

www.wpublishinggroup.com

A Division of Thomas Nelson, Inc.
www.ThomasNelson.com

I Grew Up Little

©2004 by Patsy Clairmont

Published by W Publishing Group, a Division of Thomas Nelson, Inc., P. O. Box 141000, Nashville, Tennessee 37214.

All Scripture quotations, unless otherwise indicated, are taken from *The Message* (MSG) by Eugene H. Peterson, copyright © 1993, 1994, 1995, 1996, 2000, 2001, 2002. Used by permission of NavPress Publishing Group. All rights reserved.

Other Scripture references are from the following sources:

The New King James Version (NKJV) © 1982 by Thomas Nelson, Inc.

The King James Version (KJV) and *The Holy Bible, New International Version* (NIV) © 1973, 1978, 1984, by International Bible Society. Used by permission of Zondervan Bible Publishers.

Cataloging-in-Congress Publication Data

Clairmont, Patsy.
    I grew up little : finding hope in a big God / Patsy Clairmont.
    p. cm.
    ISBN 0-8499-1810-3 (hardcover)
    1. Clairmont, Patsy.   2. Christian biography—United States.   I. Title.
    BR1725.C475A3   2004
    277.3'082'092–dc22   2003020222
                                                CIP

Printed in the United States of America
04 05 06 BVG 5 4 3 2 1

Hope is a thing with feathers

That perches in the soul

And sings the tune without the words

And never stops at all.

—EMILY DICKINSON

To Jesus for redeeming me,
To my family for enduring me,
To my grandsons, Justin and Noah, for renewing me.

Contents

Contents

Foreword

I SAT IN THE FRONT ROW of the auditorium holding the program of the evening's events and saw that I went on after the book reviews. "Why do they always feel led to have book reviews at each of these women's retreats?" I mused. "They are always so boring." I looked up at the ladies sitting in a dignified row on the platform. "Which one is going to do the reviews?" I wondered.

In the midst of these important leaders sat a little lady. She was in a plain cotton dress and flat shoes. She wore no make-up and looked out of place in this group. At that point the chairman announced "Patsy Clairmont will now give us the book reviews."

Up jumped this little person, bounced to the lectern where she barely peered over the top. As she moved to the side where we could see her, it was as though lights went on. Make-up wasn't needed as her face took on an energy of its own. She was

vii

hilarious! I'd never seen such an instant transformation before, and I approached her afterwards and invited her to come to the first CLASS I had prepared. "You have such amazing potential," I said. "Have you ever thought of becoming a speaker?" She gave me several reasons why she couldn't do this, but I invited her to join the group that included several Hollywood personalities.

The rest is history as the potential exploded into reality. She was a quick learner and she ate up the instruction as a hungry child. I feel today that if I had done nothing more than light Patsy's fire, it would have been enough.

—FLORENCE LITTAUER
Founder, The CLASSeminar
Speaker, Author of *Silver Boxes* and *Personality Plus*

1

Want Ad

JOB WANTED: *Woman seeking inspirational speaking and writing opportunities.* QUALIFICATIONS: *High school dropout, teenage runaway, and agoraphobic.*

WOULD YOU HIRE THIS WOMAN? Me either! Which is what makes my story one of hope: I was hired. Oh, not right away, of course. It took a gazillion years to move past my phobias, hang-ups, and shortcomings, and the path did plenty of zigging and zagging. But the end of the story is a happy one. Not a perfect one, but a perfectly good one.

When I was about twenty years old, I was knee-deep in emotional instability. By the time the calendar had flipped over twenty-three times, I was drowning. An addict to nicotine, caffeine, and tranquilizers, even I had to confess that my neurotic lifestyle held nothing inspirational. Add to that my obsessive fears, my repressed anger, and my unrelenting guilt, and I was unemployable in any market. As a full-blown agoraphobic (unable to leave home), I clung to the walls of my house, longing for security while smothering those I most loved with my neediness.

So how does one go from housebound to footloose and Jesus free? Folks often ask how I broke out of my prison of fears to now stand before thousands in arenas throughout the nation proclaiming a message of liberty. I can tell you it wasn't easy, quick, or without painful effort. Yet because of the hope of the Lord that flooded into my heart again and again, I took scary steps toward my recovery.

I know, I know, you thought I was going to say I became ensnared in my insecurities, then I met Jesus, and he set me free. Actually, I was a Christian throughout those troubled years, which made the mess my life was in all the more confusing for me. I couldn't figure out why God just didn't fix me. But the Lord didn't plan to stay up late one night and slipstitch my fractured parts back together. Instead, he began a holy procedure of deep, inner repair that required my involvement. It would take me years to sort out God's part and my part in the healing process. Eventually, I came to realize that God isn't a fixer, he is a redeemer. The lost are found, the blind see, the sick are healed, and the lame walk again, but each redemption requires the willingness of the redeemed to be reclaimed.

I was lost in an emotional thundercloud; I was blind to any path that might lead me out of my despair; I was mentally muddled, and my faltering walk was one of obvious dysfunction. In the following chapters, I will introduce you to the people who encircled my life, then lead you into my despairing years and, finally, out into the daylight of God's irrepressible hope.

While I wouldn't have given the woman who wrote the want ad a whit of a chance of surviving—nor did few others—the Lord took delight in providing for and eventually using her in unexpected ways.

In my journey I've learned that hope was not, as I had feared, hidden away on some other planet. For hope may arrive in a song, a phone call, an apology, a vision, a promise, a sunset, or a new day. Hope, my friends, is just a breath away.

May you find in these pages a sense that "If God would do that for her, there's hope for me," because God is big, even if we are little.

"Oh! May the God of green hope fill you up with joy, fill you up with peace, so that your believing lives, filled with the life-giving energy of the Holy Spirit, will brim over with hope!" (Romans 15:13).

Hope is just a breath away.

2
Rebecca of Rosecreek

I GREW UP LITTLE. That shouldn't have been a surprise since my mom's four-foot-ten-inch stature loomed over me throughout my life. Oh, I grew to be taller than she—I'm a full five feet—but Mom was a force to be reckoned with. She was a giant in her faith, which helped moderate the tyrant in her temperament. Mom, a tiny bundle of fireworks, exploded over her family landscape and left a dazzling impact.

Meet Becky. If you ask her, she would tell you she's Rebecca of Sunnybrook Farm. If you ask those who knew her growing up, they would tell you she was Rebecca of Rosecreek Road, Nebo, Kentucky. And if you would ask me, I'd be quick to tell you, "She's my mom," a rambunctious bundle of love, lectures, legalism, and liberty. A contradiction, as most of us are.

Born Rebecca Ann Myers, she was the youngest in a family of six children. Her mother, Ruthie Ann, died when Mom was a young teen, and her dad, Dempsey, died before I was born. Because Mom was the baby of the family, she was nicknamed "Sister" by her siblings. Being especially small for her age, she found her brothers and sisters were attentive to her needs.

Mom said growing up on a farm during the Depression was to their advantage because they always had food on the table. But they worked hard, even as children, helping with the field chores, including the tobacco crop. All the Myerses' kids hated the task of hunting for the huge worms that attacked the tobacco leaves. The children would have to move down each tobacco row, plucking the worms from the leaves and pinching off the worms' heads. Eew! Sister would dawdle down her assigned rows, knowing that if she waited long enough, her siblings would come to her rescue and complete her task.

Mom didn't talk much about her childhood and even less about her parents. I once heard one of her sisters say their dad was a severe man; the others said nothing about him.

When Mom was nineteen, she eloped with my dad, who was twenty-two, to be married by a justice of the peace. Dad was a playfully subdued personality while Mom swung between dynamo and depressed. I would learn the tobacco leaf doesn't fall far from the plant.

Mom and Dad's first home, a petite, three-room house, was two doors away from my dad's parents' house and next door to Mom's sister, Elvira. Mom and Dad had a small coal stove for heat, and in the wee hours, when the embers died out, the little dwelling froze, causing their fishbowl and gold-fish to become one solid fish-sicle. The next morning my parents would stoke up the coals, and when the house warmed, the fish would thaw and continue circling their glassy habitat.

One of my favorite stories, because it provides a window into Mom's mighty heart, occurred during Halloween, while my parents lived in that house. An adult cousin disguised herself and stepped into Mom and Dad's house. The only one in the kitchen was my toddler brother, Donnie, who was sitting in his highchair. On seeing a masked person enter the room, he began to cry. The cousin, deciding this wasn't such a good idea after all, bolted out the door and raced down the street for her house.

My mom stepped into the kitchen to see why Don was howling just in time to catch a glimpse of someone dashing out the door. Mom sped for the door in hot pursuit and, being the fleeter of the two, overtook the stranger a block away in a field and tackled her. The cousin was so breath-less from the race and subsequent laughter as they scuffled that she couldn't identify herself to Mom before her mask was ripped off. Once my mom discovered who it was, they had a lively chuckle together, but my feisty little mom had made it clear she wasn't about to let any home intruder escape.

Mom's humor surprised me one day when I was fifteen years old. I had just washed my hands in the kitchen sink and was searching for a dishtowel to dry my hands when Mom walked through carrying a load of freshly folded quilts. Feeling fairly safe because her arms were full, I flicked the water from my hands at her, not anticipating her playful response. Before I knew what had happened, Mom dropped the quilts, corralled my head in her arm, and galloped me to the sink, where I got an ample dousing. We both laughed ourselves silly.

I have a framed picture of my mom as an adult riding a child's tricycle. I've always loved that photograph because it captured the lighthearted side of her that often was squelched by life's intensity.

The Depression sent many Southerners scrambling north for work; my parents and brother were part of that scramble. In 1939 they settled in Detroit, where my dad became a milkman for Sealtest.

I was born on April 3, 1945, nine years and ten days after my brother. Mom was committed to making me into Shirley Temple, but I was definitely more Calamity Jane. Oh, I enjoyed the wardrobe of costumes and outfits Mom made for me, but I was resistant to getting "cleaned up." Hair snarls and mud splats made Mom's eyes roll in disapproval while I felt they gave me a lived-in look. From as young as I can remember, Mom was training me to be a "little lady," and I was stretching her patience with my dirty-face reality.

I'm sure part of her frustration was that she was fastidious in her personal appearance and home—unless she was in a slump. Her emotional downs weren't frequent but, because they stood out in such contrast to her usual sunshiny behavior, they were memorable. During Mom's bouts with depression, I remember the house seeming dark, sad, and askew, and her being withdrawn.

Usually, though, our home sparkled with her diligent efforts. She was a cross between Betty Crocker, Heloise, and Martha Stewart. Innovative, creative, and motivated, my petite mom would tackle almost any job, including rooftops, wall demolition, furniture upholstery, and landscaping.

Mom knew how to take the extra steps to transform ordinary into exceptional. Whether she whipped up a meal, decorated a room, threw a party, taught a class, or sported an outfit, Mom excelled in presentation. Her finishing efforts made her crystal gleam, her throw rugs fluff, her pillows poof, her flowers bloom, her mirrors sparkle, her cupboards arrange, her food delight, and her guests cheer.

But Mom's perfectionism kept her frustrated and those of us who lived with her tense. Her Saturday housecleaning was more like other people's spring-cleaning. I can remember debating with her as a teenager why I had to scrub all the baseboards on my knees and strip the wax off the kitchen floor every weekend.

Even though Mom retained high standards, a definite change in her demands on herself and others occurred when I was nine years old. Two adults arrived each week to visit with Mom. I never got to know them because I always was sent outside while they were there.

Then one day they never came back again. Later I learned that Mom had been on a personal quest for hope and that she had been studying with Jehovah's Witnesses. Mom had just enough background in Sunday school from her childhood that she found herself in constant disagreement with the Witnesses' theology. Even though they stopped coming by, Mom continued to pore over the Scriptures in search of answers. Then a neighbor, who had been taking me to Sunday school, invited Mom to attend. She accepted not only the invitation but also, a short time later, Christ as her Savior. She was forever changed.

Mom embraced her new faith with the same zeal as she cleaned house. Instead of her driving perfectionism wearing her nerves and ours thin, Mom was more settled and satisfied. Oh, she still wanted things tidy, but now instead of being frantic in her efforts, you could hear her newfound hope in the hymns she sang as she cleaned. "In the Garden," "What a Friend We Have in Jesus," and "The Old Rugged Cross" wafted down the halls of our home daily. Of course, I still had to help with chores on Saturdays (rats!), but Mom became overly lenient regarding my bedroom. But that's another story we would need a backhoe to venture into.

As she grew in her faith and grace, we, her family, were usually the recipients. We noticed Mom was less radical when we messed up. She was steadier in her emotions, which made home feel safer, and she was quieter at her core, which made her feel safer. While Mom never was physically abusive, her temper was intimidating enough to make us all quake. When she would rail on and on about my misdeeds, I can remember thinking, *I wish she would just hit me and be done with it.* Today I realize I had a sensitive nature that just couldn't bear her threatening displeasure. Yet I was also an obstinate child who needed a parent with strength and determination. (Hmm, sounds like Mom was in a no-win role.)

Mom was stylish and loved shopping for clothes. But some of my sweetest memories of her center on fragrances. Her thick, wavy, blond hair smelled of Breck shampoo while she sashayed around leaving To a Wild Rose scent in her path. Our home was fragrant too, as she aired the house regularly, scrubbed the interior with pine cleaners, and used big, fat wick deodorizers throughout the rooms.

A fragrant memory I treasure is of my mom hanging clothes on the line to absorb the outdoor freshness. Her little frame, clothed in a tidy shirtwaist dress, stretched to reach the clotheslines. Wooden clothespins filled her apron pockets while a few were clamped between her teeth. She deftly emptied the contents of her woven baskets onto the lines with the skill that comes only from experience. When the clotheslines were full, the sheets waved in the perfumed breeze, promising her family a night of summer dreams.

But I think the best smell was Mom's cooking. Nobody, I mean nobody, could beat her Southern fried chicken, baking powder biscuits, gravy, and banana pudding.

Still, one of my favorite remembrances of Mom is more reflective. Some days I'd walk into a room and see her with her Bible spread out in her lap searching the Scriptures. I now have her Bible, but I don't use it because she wore it out. It's a loose pile of pages with a detached, tattered leather cover that has a golden sketch of Christ shepherding sheep on it.

Mom knew about sheep, especially straying ones. My brother, sister, and I all had extended seasons of rebellion toward her and the Lord. We thought she had too many rules and her standards were too high for us to attain. And each of us believed we could handle life without the help of her God. We were wrong. I'm grateful that the Lord heard our mother's fervent prayers, and he had mercy on us. Each of us eventually gave our sin-sick hearts to the Lord Jesus, and we thanked him that he and our mom never gave up on us. Hope keeps a mother's light glowing.

In 1977, when Mom was sixty-two, I began to notice some changes in her. At first I couldn't put my finger on what was different except that she was more demanding and often seemed offended by other's innocuous actions. She seemed gradually to be losing her pliability, her characteristic humility, and her song.

Then one day she became confused about the voices on the radio and thought they were people I was talking to. That frightened me. After that strange incident I became vigilant around her, watching her behavior, but she seemed fine. I tucked away that scary moment and had almost forgotten it when, a few years later, Mom had outbursts of anger about things that before wouldn't have bothered her.

I told myself that when folks age they become cranky. Mom became forgetful, but then, I thought, so did I. I also noted paranoia slipping in, with Mom layering Band-Aids over the peephole on her apartment door because she believed people were spying on her. But then I thought, *If it makes her feel safer, why not cover it?* I made many concessions for her because I so wanted my mom to be all right.

Mom started walking, which at first I thought was great exercise for her, but then I noticed it became more of a compulsion than a pleasure. One day she decided to walk to an area drive-through restaurant, two miles away, to buy some hamburgers. That would have been fine, but she had to walk beside a major thoroughfare and under a bridge without the safety of sidewalks, and that wasn't okay. Then, instead of walking beside the busy highway, Mom hiked along on the edge of the road with cars whisking past at high speeds. A man, seeing my little mom toddling along, pulled up by her and insisted she get in the car with him, which she did. He was an angel in disguise, not only taking Mom to the restaurant but also dropping her off at her home and making her promise she would never do that again. As she recounted her adventure to me, I realized that, if my mom were reasoning correctly, she never would have walked where she did, and she certainly wouldn't have accepted a ride from a stranger.

"Mom," I bellowed. "What were you thinking? Why, that man could have hurt you!"

"Oh, I was ready for him." She balled up her mosquito-sized fist.

Then I realized I was the mom and she was my rebellious teenager who didn't understand the ramifications of her choices.

That episode was quickly followed by a number of other threatening events. One evening I arrived at her apartment when she was preparing her dinner.

"Hi, Mom. How are you?"

"Fine." She smiled as she greeted me.

"What's that smell?" I hotfooted it for her kitchen.

"It's just my dinner heating up," she called after me.

I opened the oven to find Mom was warming her dinner on a smoldering paper plate that was about to burst into flames. I quickly remedied the situation but realized she no longer could distinguish between the functions of the microwave and the stove. We unplugged Mom's oven to limit her use to the microwave, but we knew that was a temporary solution.

Sometimes Mom's changing behavior was unexpectedly childlike and comical. One day she called and asked me to come over because she had "a little something" for me. I was involved in some project and told her I'd have to stop by the following day. Well, she didn't want to wait so she loaded up the "little something" into her grocery cart and began the trek over to my house.

I was standing at the kitchen sink, when I looked out the window and spotted a shopping cart wobbling toward me over the stones in the road. The "something" in the cart had enough stature to hide the cart's driver. It looked like an apparition-driven cart because the gift Mom was delivering was a three-foot, illuminated, plastic ghost. Uh-huh, a ghost. No, I don't know why Mom figured I needed Casper, except that she thought I would get a kick out of him. And I did. Not because of what the gift was, but because Mom was so cute in her determination to make a home delivery. Her mile-long walk through the middle of town must have caused whiplash for a number of observers.

At a certain point in Mom's journey into Alzheimer's, she all but forgot how to be difficult; she became the sweetest gal you would ever want to meet. She was compassionate, tender, and loving. Oh, she still has a few unpleasant moments, but most of the time she is a joy.

With her mind clouding over, we knew we would have to make arrangements for her supervision before she toddled herself into danger. But before we could act, Mom paid a six-week visit to my sister, Elizabeth, in Florida and never came back. My sister and her family decided they wanted to keep Mom and care for her themselves. What a sweet, generous answer to prayer.

Mom, who is now eighty-seven, has lived with Elizabeth's family for six years, and Elizabeth told me her greatest fear is Mom's dying. Elizabeth said Mom has brought so much love to their home, as well as team spirit because it takes the whole family to care for her, that to lose Mom would be a great deprivation.

Elizabeth and I chat regularly, and she updates me on Mom and their latest escapades. But Mom doesn't wander away anymore because her legs no longer work. The doctors say there is no medical reason, just that Mom's brain has forgotten how to walk.

Her cognitive times usually last only minutes. Mom calls my sister, "Hey, lady," and she spends most of her day praying a little singsong prayer: "This I pray every day and a good night and a good day and amen. Take us up to be with you, our family and friends, and a good night and a good day and amen."

Last year Elizabeth was diagnosed with breast cancer. The jolt of that news left her rattled, and to complicate matters, her husband was in Korea for a year with the Air Force. Elizabeth's children were too young to comprehend the devastation of her diagnosis or to know how to comfort her, and our mom was in her own shrouded world. Overwhelmed by her sense of aloneness, my sister could hear despair knocking on her heart's door.

Then Elizabeth recounted to me the following events: "I walked into the living room, dragging my heavy heart, when Mom called to me, 'Hey, lady; hey, lady.'"

Beth slowly made her way across the room to Mom's side.

"C'mere." Mom motioned with her hand for Elizabeth to bend down near her.

Elizabeth leaned down to see what Mom wanted when Mom wrapped her hands around Beth's neck and drew her closer. Then Mom beseeched God on Beth's behalf, "I pray the Lord will give you the strength you will need to go through the days ahead. May you sense his presence and rest in his love. In Jesus' name, amen."

"Elizabeth," I squealed, when she told me the story, "that was a miracle! Mom prayed for you and in such a focused and relevant way."

"I know, I know. If ever I needed to hear our mom's prayers, it was then."

"What did you do after she prayed?"

"I cried and cried. And afterward I felt hopeful, like I could face whatever was ahead."

"How long has it been since Mom prayed for you specifically?"

"Years. Many years."

What can I say? Mom, you continue to dazzle us.

Hope Keeps a Mother's
Candle Glowing

3
Mac the Milkman

"GOT MILK?" While that's a clever advertising slogan, it was never a question when I was growing up. Mac the Milkman was my dad. When I think about my dad, I think about the sounds that represent different refrains in our relationship.

If you're old enough to remember the sound of milk bottles being placed into your milk chute, then you're from my generation. I can still hear the bottles' glassy song as my dad swung wooden crates full of clattering milk containers into the back of his Divco milk truck. On occasion I helped Dad fill his milk carriers with his customers' orders, which could include cottage cheese, ice cream, whipping cream, sour cream, and sometimes bread and eggs. He was a full-service milkman. In fact, many of Dad's customers told him where their house keys were hidden so he could place the orders right in their refrigerators.

I loved everything about my dad being a Sealtest milk-man. I even adored the toe-tapping jingle, "Get the best, get the best, get Sealtest." I thought home milk delivery a wholesome occupation, which of course, provided us with a constant flow of fresh dairy products. And once Dad bought a milk route in our neighborhood, he could swing by home for lunch. I thought that friendly.

Mac, my dad's nickname, wasn't much of a conversationalist. He was pleasant but not invested in meaningful exchanges. He was quick to smile, mellow, and usually tired. He didn't seem terribly passionate about life . . . well, maybe fishing. Dad was, however, committed to napping. He required a lot of rest, and his idea of sports (beyond dropping a line in the water or snoring under a newspaper) was a crossword puzzle. When he couldn't figure out an answer, he made up his own word and crammed it in the boxes. That made me giggle.

I remember only one time that Dad disagreed with Mom in my presence. I was twelve, and I wanted to walk to the dime store five blocks away, but my mom thought it might be dark before I could get back.

"No, Rebecca, I think it would be fine," I heard my dad say.

Now, while that might not sound like a big deal, it was colossal, a historic moment in the McEuen household. My mom must have been shocked as well because she let me go.

I skipped halfway to the store out of sheer joy that my dad

took my side and that he actually won against "she who was meant to be obeyed." Mom was definitely not the type to back-pedal on her decisions, even if it meant she could find a smoother path. I'm not sure if Dad's effort to speak up was too exhausting for him or if he paid a hefty price once I left for the store, but I never heard him disagree with her again. However, I'm certain he did in private because I can remember enduring some pretty icy days, signaling my parents were on the outs.

I think Dad was resigned to the rule of strong women. He may have been relieved they took the initiative, even at the cost of his freedom, because he needed to reserve his ebbing energies for daily tasks. Dad's mother, known to me as Mamaw, was a proper Southern lady. She was poor as a church mouse, yet full of pride. Mamaw drew straight lines for her children and required absolute obedience. She prepared the way for my straight-line mom to enter my dad's life and take over the next shift of managing Mac.

Dad was born Smith Waller McEuen. (Mamaw named Dad after the doctor who birthed him—Dr. Waller Smith.) No wonder he was exhausted. Try explaining that handle.

Folks would ask, "Sir, what is your first name?"

"Smith," Dad would answer.

"No, sir, your first name."

"Smith," he would repeat.

"Sir," they would say with a deep sigh, "I need your first name."

"That is my first name. Smith."

"What is your middle name, sir?"

"Waller."

"Walter?"

"No, Waller."

"Waller?" they would ask.

"Yes, like a pig wallers in mud."

I heard Dad run through that rigmarole over and over throughout the years in an attempt to identity himself. My dad was one of four children born to my grandparents, William Franklin McEuen and Thanie Elizabeth McEuen, residents of Madisonville, Kentucky. Dad's dad went by Frank. I called him Papaw. Throughout my childhood, I might have heard Papaw say a dozen words but probably less.

Papaw liked to rock, read the paper, and chew tobacco. He kept a rusty can nearby that he used to, ahem, deposit fluid wads in. He sipped his coffee out of a saucer, covered his food with a quarter-inch blanket of salt, and ate his peas off his knife. Papaw kept his change tucked deep inside an old, leather coin pouch. On a couple of occasions he extracted a coin or two and placed them carefully in my hand to buy a soda. Those were the most personal exchanges I had with him. He didn't speak in the exchanges, but he gave me something of his own and he touched my hand . . . and that stayed with me. He died when I was nine.

Mamaw called the shots until Papaw's death, when beyond the grave he made one strong statement. In the legal papers Papaw left behind, he had a clause that said Mamaw could live in their tiny family dwelling (five hundred square feet) for as long as she lived. But she could never sell it. It was to be sold after her death, and the monies divided among his six grandchildren. I guess Papaw, just once, wanted to have a say in something.

I don't remember hearing my dad speak of his childhood, his parents, his siblings, or his work. Did I mention he didn't say much? Yet compared to Papaw, my dad was a real chatterbox. I never saw my grandfather smile, but my dad was generous with his smiles and light laughter. I do have a picture of Papaw sitting in front of a woodshed with my dad, who was half-grown, lying over Papaw's lap, as if Papaw was going to spank Dad. It's a playful picture with a hint of a smile on Papaw's face. I framed that picture and hung it in my home. It gave me hope that maybe they had had a relationship.

Most of my growing up years, Dad wore overalls, his standard work outfit, and he always had a pocketful of change. His coins were his music; he would jingle them. I think they were sweet music to his ears after having been penny-poor through the Depression. He never told me, but I found out that, among other things, he dug ditches for the state to earn money that I'm certain was turned over to his mother to help with the groceries. I doubt that he had enough coins left in his pocket to make music with and very little reason to dance.

Throughout my rearing, Dad sporadically did a little

dance that never failed to make me chuckle. It was his condensed version of the jitterbug. It only lasted thirty seconds, but it was long enough to delight me.

Dad also played the harmonica. My favorite "tune" was when he made the harmonica sound like a locomotive. He would start off puffing into it slow and then gradually increase the speed, as if the train were pulling out of a depot and picking up steam. Then, to my delight, he would end with a long, high-pitched whistle.

My dad told me that the way birds stayed dry in the rain was by standing between the raindrops and that, if I put salt on a bird's tail, I could catch it. He had several nonsensical comments and songs that became his repertoire and my sweet remembrances.

Often, when I would ask him for something, usually money, Dad would quip, "You talk like a woman with a paper head." And he regularly informed me that, "Folks act funny when it comes to their money." I wore a ponytail for years, and Dad would sing, "Horse-y put your tail up, put your tail up, put your tail up, horse-y put your tail up, and keep the sun out of my eyes." But my favorite songs he would sing were "You Are My Sunshine" and a short ditty about "K-K-K-Katie."

"K-K-K-Katie, K-K-K Katie, you're the only g-g-g-girl that I adore. When the m-moon shines over the cow shed, I'll be waiting at the k-k-k-kitchen door."

When I was twelve, my mom and I were baptized in a

church at the end of our street. I remember I shook like a
leaf, fearing the immersion process, but even of greater con-
cern was whether my dad would come to watch. (Dad wasn't
a churchgoer.) It wasn't until I trembled my way down the
steps into the deep waters of the baptistery that I caught a
glimpse of him sitting near the front. I wasn't afraid anymore.

For years I was my dad's bright light, but as I grew older
and required as much as I gave relationally, he backed away. I
remember as a little girl my dad fussing over me when my
mom would dress me up. He would clap and sing, "Ain't She
Sweet," and for the moment I would feel validated and loved.
But when I was in my early teens, he couldn't deal with my
growing moods, and I felt his emotional departure as clear as
if he had shut a door in my face.

Only once do I remember my dad physically getting
tough with me. I was a teenager, and he told me to get in the
car. I said I wouldn't, and he grabbed my arm and began to
force me toward the door. I pulled loose and got in on my
own, but I was surprised and shaken by the handprint on my
arm. I couldn't decide if his action meant he despised me or
loved me. Dad had never been that strong or involved in my
discipline so I wasn't certain where to file within me his
abrupt behavior. I acted like I resented his sudden intrusion,
but even more it scared me. Not enough that I wanted to
obey (too little, too late), but enough that I purposed to
avoid him. Dad didn't seem to mind.

That left me emotionally estranged from both of my parents. A condition not unknown to teens, but for relationally hungry me, the situation created a hole of need in my heart.

I married Les right after my seventeenth birthday. Dad liked him a lot. After the ceremony Dad told Les, as he pumped his hand, "I wish you a lot more luck with Patsy than we've had." Yup, I would have been a handful for hearty parents, but for my laid-back, easygoing, noncommunicative dad, I was overwhelming.

Years later God channeled my overwhelming need to talk into a speaking ministry. But my dad heard me speak before a group only once before he died, and that was for five minutes at an Easter sunrise service held at a nearby youth camp. When I mentioned I had been asked to share "How I Know Jesus Lives," Dad announced he would attend. I was stunned. Dad had never volunteered to attend church in his life—aside from the day I was baptized.

When I awoke that Easter morning to sheets of ice covering our roadways, my heart sank. I had so wanted Dad to come. I longed for his validation and was thrilled to think he would be in church after a lifetime of being absent. Les and I didn't live far from the camp; so we slid over to the facility, but my parents had to negotiate fifteen miles of winding road. Just moments before the service began I looked up, and in walked my parents. After I gave my little talk, I sat down and looked at my dad. His eyes were full of tears. I was moved because Dad didn't show emotions beyond laughter or displeasure. He never said anything about my talk, but he didn't have to—those tears were enough.

Some months later my dad was diagnosed with prostate cancer. Mom called to tell me. Later that day Dad dropped by my home. He didn't say anything about the dreadful diagnosis so I brought it up. Dad had a hard time repeating what the doctor had told him.

I remember feeling terribly sad for him, yet I didn't express it aloud. I didn't even hug him. Perhaps because it hadn't been our way to talk about important matters, and the awkwardness of this life-and-death issue was too difficult a place for us to begin.

In the two years that followed, as Dad's health slipped away, he became snippy with everyone. We all understood he was in pain and frustrated, and we usually extended him grace. Occasionally we snapped back and then instantly regretted it. Toward the end of his life, the cancer moved into his bones.

One day Dad dropped by my home without Mom, something that had happened only half a dozen times in my adult life. He handed me a napkin full of seeds and three tiny pieces of driftwood. He told me he had harvested the seeds off a bush with lovely flowers in his backyard because he thought I might enjoy growing one. The small wood pieces were very smooth and unusual, and he said he didn't know what one could do with them, but he thought if anyone would know, it would be me.

I was speechless. I don't remember my dad ever picking

out a gift for me. I was touched that he had collected those seeds and equally surprised that he thought I was creative. That was eighteen years ago, and I still have those wrapped seeds and the handful of wood.

One month before Dad died, while in his hospital bed with Mom at his side, he gave his heart to Christ. They took communion together; Dad's first and only time. When I arrived at his bedside, Mom told me of Dad's conversion. I stood at the foot of his bed and quoted Jesus's words, "In my Father's house are many mansions; if it were not so, I would have told you. I go to prepare a place for you. And if I go and prepare a place for you, I will come again and receive you to Myself; that where I am, there you may be also" (John 14:2–3 NKJV). Hope is hearing "today you will be with Me in Paradise" (Luke 23:43 NKJV).

Almost four weeks later, I had a dream that Mamaw was seated on the end of Dad's bed weeping and that my father had only two days before he would die. When I awoke, I was certain I needed to rush to his bedside; so Les and I made the hour and a half drive to the hospital. On the way, we hit black ice and found ourselves slipping and sliding until we arrived at the hospital. I was frightened, especially because I didn't like car trips of any kind to begin with; so we didn't stay long with my dad. Besides, he looked better than he had, and I figured my dream was nothing but an expression of my anxiety. When we left the hospital, Dad was disappointed that we were going so soon.

That was Sunday. Early Tuesday (two days later), the call came from my sobbing mother that Dad had died.

Nothing prepares you to step into a roomful of coffins. To walk the aisles among them, deciding which one is right for your loved one, is surreal. At one point the director showed us an elegant coffin. I said, "Sir, this appears to be the Cadillac version, and my mom has a Volkswagen purse. Could we look at those?" I helped Mom with the selection, and we moved on with the rest of the plans. The service was a small gathering of family and friends held at the funeral home.

Dad wasn't an ambitious man, which meant he also had no propensity toward greediness or manipulation. It wasn't his way to speak against people or to deliberately cause trouble. He liked to laugh and rest. Even his food was simple: A biscuit torn into chunks, dropped into a tall glass, and covered in buttermilk satisfied his palate. He loved Mom and was quietly proud when his kids made good choices. He liked finding throwaway treasures. (Mom put her foot down, though, when he dragged home a ladder with only two rungs.) He liked to doodle cartoon figures on the back of napkins or envelopes, listen to Kate Smith sing, "When the Moon Comes over the Mountain," work on his whistling skills, whittle on wood, and sip black coffee.

The concert of songs from the milk bottles, the whistle of the harmonica, and the tunes he offered still sing in my heart as a sweet communication of love and goodwill. I miss him.

———— ✦ ————

Hope is hearing
"Today you will be with Me in Paradise."

4

Lucky Strikes and Dentyne Gum

When you're a nine-year-old boy, a sister is not on your wish list. A puppy, yes. A snake, maybe. But a sister, never! Yet there I was: one chubby, blue-eyed blonde altering my brother Don's only-child lifestyle. Don was nine years old when I was born, and he was well adjusted to being numero uno. While my parents were tickled pink at my girlish entrance, my brother was tinged with shades of blue. Our colorful beginning would turn into years mixed with sweetness and sadness.

One of my favorite childhood pictures is of Don, with his blond, wavy hair, and me, with my blond hair slicked back into a ponytail. Perhaps I like it because we had so few photographs of us taken together. Or maybe it's because I believe everyone should have a big brother to protect her from bullies and to reach high stuff and to hold her hand crossing streets.

I loved that Don was my brother because he was playful and dear, but to be quite honest, I didn't fully appreciate those qualities until he was out of the house and off on his own. Prior to his leaving to join the armed services, Don and I were often a tangle of sibling rivalry. We had agreeable moments and endearing times offset by highly seasoned spats. Don had the dubious position of being not only brotherly toward me but also parental. Our age difference bred that positioning as well as the expectations of our parents, who didn't always have the emotional energy to invest in caring for me.

Each passing year our sibling struggles grew more intense. When Don wanted to ride bikes with the boys, he was sidelined helping Mom with me. When he entered high school and began to date, Don had to make his plans around babysitting me. Before he left for school each morning, he had to make sure I was dressed, fed, and out the door on time as well. None of these big-brother adjustments endeared me to him.

Of course, the indulgences my parents tossed my way didn't win me any points with Don—not that I was trying to earn any. I had double-barreled childish attitudes displayed in bouts of pouting and whining. Winsome I wasn't. Don grew tired of home rules and downright resentful that he had me as a constant appendage; so when he was old enough to leave home, he did.

I "left home" the first time when I was almost three years old. I locked myself in the bathroom, much to my delight and everyone else's consternation. My parents tried, to no avail, to talk me into opening the door. The bathroom window was too high and small to get to me; so their only hope was negotiating with a determined toddler. I was enjoying all the people-energy my entrapment was generating, and I was in no hurry to let everyone settle down. Finally the compassionate pleas of my twelve-year-old brother convinced me I should step out of my self-imposed isolation. Don was touted as the hero for weeks afterward, but that was only one of a thimbleful of amiable moments I can remember from my childhood.

One holiday, when I was six and Don was fifteen, Mom, exasperated at our ongoing bickering, bought two Christmas trees, one for each of us to be placed on either side of the fireplace. This was to keep us from battling over who got to hang what where, but Mom claims instead we bickered over whose tree was prettier, wider, taller, and greener. And green was often the color of our perspective of each other. We even found glee in the other one "catching it" from Mom.

One day I came home from school and found my preteen brother filling the bathtub with milk. He had heard it was good for your skin and decided to immerse himself, but Don hadn't calculated how much milk it would take to fill a tub so he ended up with more of a foot-splash. When our conservative mom found out Don had literally dumped gallons of milk down the drain, she was less than homogenized in her response. Personally, I found the whole scenario entertaining.

Don had his own way of entertaining himself. In fact, to my chagrin, he introduced me early on to the game fifty-two-pick-up, which is exactly what I had to do after he bent a deck of cards and then let them fly, scattering them willy-nilly around the room for me to retrieve. Don also taught me how to build houses with playing cards, which I spent hours constructing until he would walk by and topple them with a single breath. Yep, he knew where I parked my goat, but every once in a while I'd think up a scheme of my own.

I was eight and Don was seventeen, when I was assigned the bedmaking duty one particular Saturday morning. The problem was Don was sound asleep in his bed, preventing me from completing my tasks. Then I came up with a brilliant plan. I took the receiver off the hook, ran into his room, shook his arm, and told him his girlfriend was on the phone. He leapt out of the bed like a launching rocket ship, and while he sprinted toward the phone in the dining room, I quickly made his bed, which is when my plan began to unravel. I hadn't taken into consideration what would happen when Don picked up the receiver and was greeted by an empty line. Let's just say I didn't use that approach again.

On rare occasions Don would leave me speechless. One Saturday my mom told me that Don and his girlfriend, Carole, were going to take me ice-skating with them. I remember my disbelief. I stared at my mom wondering why she would make up such a tale, when we all knew Don never volunteered to take me anywhere. Then Mom presented me with a beautiful new pair of white ice skates, and I began to believe her. Even as Don, Carole, and I pulled away from the house, I expected someone to yell, "April Fool." I was unusually subdued during that outing, jolted, I think, by the unexpected inclusion.

It's funny what ends up being sweet memories. You know, the ones that make you feel a part of another person's life. One season Don played Johnny Ray's records "Cry" and the "Little White Cloud That Cried" repeatedly; I still remember most of the words. At the time, I couldn't imagine why anyone would want to hear the same songs over and over. But when I hit my teenage years, I understood Don's "love song" behavior. I continually played "Are you Lonesome Tonight?" by Elvis and sighed over the drama of life.

Another pleasing memory for me from Don's teen years was his habit of emptying his pockets onto the living room's chartreuse leather end table with the oriental, fringed lamp before he headed to bed. In the morning before he awoke, I loved fingering through his stash. It always included pieces of Dentyne gum (which I helped myself to) amidst a sea of coins, a Zippo lighter, and his Lucky Strike cigarettes. His pocketful of paraphernalia became a pocketful of memories for me.

Don joined the Army the same month he turned eighteen and initially was stationed at Fort Bragg, North Carolina. His overseas assignment was with the 101st Airborne in Germany, where he was stationed for more than two years.

By the time he and Carole, who was now his wife, returned to the States, they had two darling little girls, Debbie and Cheryl. Eventually they added Susan, Donald, Steven, and Scott to complete their family. I thought the gift of becoming an aunt to six beautiful children was one of the sweetest things my brother had done for me.

During one difficult season of his life, he needed a job but was having trouble finding work. He heard that the Ford Motor Company was hiring, but the lines for applicants were long when he arrived. Desperate to have a paycheck to feed his big family, he climbed the fence in the back to bypass the crowds. The guards caught him and tossed him out.

Undeterred, Don scaled the fence again, and once again he was caught. This time, as the guards were ushering him out, Don quipped, "My Uncle Henry won't like this!" It tickled the guards that Don would suggest he was related to Henry Ford, and they decided to let him in.

But when he made his way to the hiring room, they announced all positions were taken and that he could go home. Don sat down. The man repeated, "You can go home now."

"Nope," Don replied, "I have six children, and I can't go home until I have a job. So I'll just wait here."

After several circular conversations, the man rifled back through his papers and found Don a job, much to everyone's relief. Don worked there for many years.

My brother's adult nickname, Fuzzy, came from his lack

of locks. He didn't seem to mind the nickname; perhaps because he kept a full arsenal of handles for others. For instance, when we were growing up, he called me Squirt and Short Stuff.

Don and I set aside rivalry as adults and became friends, and we never had a single argument once we made peace with each other. But sadly our personal struggles and family responsibilities prevented us from really knowing each other. Don's battle with alcohol and mine with agoraphobia kept us in unhealthy, restrictive cycles. Oh, we got together, especially at holiday time, but we didn't talk about our pain, losses, dreams, or hopes.

But I was always pleased to see him. Don had a wonderful smile and a spunky sense of humor. He was kind and truly endearing. During our adult years he called me his "big, little sister"—*big* because I was the older sister and *little* because I was a pipsqueak.

Don enjoyed my husband and was kind to my children but kept a distance from meaningful involvement. However, he was willing to exchange endless fishing stories with anyone who would bite.

One spring day in 1974 I answered the telephone, and to my surprise, my brother announced, "I've been saved."

I replied, "Saved from what?"

"My sin," he responded.

I was floored. As a family, we had been praying for years for this moment, but I was having trouble comprehending that it had happened. Don went on to say that he had joined a Bible study, had a Bible with his name on it, and was going to be baptized on Sunday, and would I come down for the service. Stampeding horses couldn't have kept me away.

When I hung up, I sprinted through the campgrounds where we lived and worked to tell my husband. I remember how exhilarated I felt. I wanted to skip, shout, and sing all at the same time. Hope, like spring, arrives fragrant with new life.

Ten months later a phone call came in the middle of the night. My sister-in-law told us that my brother had been in a car accident. Les had answered the phone out of a deep sleep and mumbled to me that Don had broken his leg. It wouldn't be until morning that I would learn that Don was in a coma with extensive injuries and that he might not live.

At the hospital the family members were allowed to go in two people at a time only once an hour for five minutes, and there were no chairs in the room. As Les and I made our way down the corridor to see Don, I heard a voice behind me say, "You can't do that."

I turned and saw a nurse pointing at my fifteen-year-old niece, Susan, who had pulled a rolling chair away from a nursing station and was pushing it down the hall toward Don's room. When the nurse called out to her, Susan jutted out her chin and stated through tears and grit, "I am going to kiss my daddy."

Susan pushed the chair past us and into Don's room and over to his bedside. The bed was set up high, and Don was attached to life-support equipment. Susan carefully made her way up the side of the bed, through the life-support paraphernalia, and sweetly kissed her comatose daddy. It was the only way she had left to tell him she loved him.

Don would be diagnosed as brain dead, and five days after his accident, he would officially be pronounced dead.

He was just over a month away from his thirty-ninth birthday. I can still see in my mind's eye Don's six children placing favorite items of his in the casket to show their affection and as a way of saying good-bye—his favorite fishing rod, his cowboy hat, his pipe, and more.

The news of Don's accident and condition so profoundly affected our mom that upon hearing it, a blood vessel in her eye burst, and when she stood up, her hip went out of place, which had never happened before. At one point during the hospital vigil my passive dad had to be assisted outside into the fresh air because he thought he was going to collapse. Several times at the funeral home I had to lift my distraught mom off the casket and help her back to a chair.

Month after month passed, and we all ached over Don's death, as each family member dealt with the loss differently. Some withdrew, others busied themselves; some talked about their feelings, others buried theirs. I personally had never felt pain that piercing. My heart was so heavy it took all my strength to move from one room to another, and it was difficult to breathe deeply.

At first I thought about Don hourly, then gradually the

agony lessened, and I found I could think about him without it wrenching my heart. However, I did come to realize that along with the loss I was also carrying a heart-load of guilt. Don and I had minimal contact that year as daily busyness and procrastination had eaten up my intentions to call him or to pay a visit. Don and his family lived a thirty-minute drive away, which seemed far and inconvenient at the time, but after his death, I realized how simple it would have been to jump in the car and go. While I have forgiven myself, I will always carry a cupful of sadness inside my heart for what could have been. And there will always be a sibling space of longing for my big brother.

Even though it probably would have made Don uncomfortable, I wish I had expressed my love to him. I believe he knew, but I should have told him. He deserved to hear.

I think my brother, like our dad, would have been content with a cabin on a lake, a motorboat, and a supply of tackle. Oh, wait. Throw in a porch swing for my nap-taking dad, a cabinetful of spicy foods for Don, and a deck of cards to wile away their evening hours. While neither of them would have made a good hermit and they both loved their families, they just didn't require a lot to make them happy— unlike Don's big little sister, who was clueless as to what would make her happy. . . .

Hope, like spring,
arrives fragrant with new life.

5

Baby Doll

I was almost nine and a half when my mom gave me a long, gift-wrapped box for Christmas. I quickly pulled the paper off the present and lifted the lid in anticipation. It was just as I had suspected and exactly what I wanted: a doll. When given the opportunity, I was a feisty linebacker in our neighborhood and could tackle with the best of them, yet I loved my dolls. I owned several, and a couple of them were my dear friends: Toni, a brunette whom you could give home permanents; and Dydee, a lovable baby doll who blew bubbles and wet her diaper. Dydee was, as the kids say today, way cool.

The new arrival was a show-stopper, a red-haired bride doll touting a pearl necklace and bracelet. Mom told me all the doll's clothes had been hand designed, including her hoop slip and lacy garter. Mom emphasized that the doll was very special. Have you noticed that "special" is often a setup for moms to lower the boom? Mom then announced that this was to be my last doll because, in her words, I was now "too old."

Too old? Too old? Why, I was still wearing undershirts and Mary Janes with lacy anklets and consuming Baby Huey comic books. Suddenly I didn't like this red-haired whippet of a doll, this intruder, this gown-clad demarcation between childhood and a job at the dime store. I was not ready for a last doll.

I still own that doll, and as the years have stockpiled into half a century, she has remained in her box waiting for a playmate. Fat chance. At some point she must have been in a damp environment because during a move I lifted her lid, and she looked a bit jaundiced, and her red wig had detached from her head and had slid sideways. She looked loopy. I sneered. Too old my foot!

Oh, I forgave Mom. Honest. But not totally until I was thirteen. That was when Mom presented me with a sister, Elizabeth Ann. She was even better than Dydee because all her orifices worked, and like Toni, you could fix baby Beth's thick hair in all sorts of outrageous styles. I had been the "only" child for four years—since Don had joined the army—and I was ready for company, especially in the form of a baby doll.

Mom spent months preparing Beth's fairy-tale nursery. The mint green walls, the corresponding carousel mural that covered a wall across from her crib, and a wind-up carousel lamp that played lullabies as it turned. The mint, ball-fringed café curtains allowed the afternoon sun to dance around the room, and while the nursery wasn't huge, in my eyes, it was perfect.

Mom was forty-three when she gave birth to my sister. It had been years since she had been in labor with me so she worked especially hard on her diet and exercised regularly, realizing that her risk factors were greater at that stage of her life. But her delivery went without a hitch. In fact, she said it was the easiest of all her children, and she brought home a healthy baby girl.

I bonded with Elizabeth immediately, which created a shift in our family dynamics. As a baby, Beth fought bedtime; so our parents would let her cry herself to sleep. I would sit on the floor outside Elizabeth's room and weep because they wouldn't let me go in to comfort her.

Elizabeth grew to be a mix between a Barbie doll and GI Joe. She had gorgeous, cascading hair and a need to scale high places. Even as a baby, she was quite an acrobat. She would hoist herself over the railing of her crib and up onto her Bathinette. She would traverse the Bathinette until the chest of drawers was in leaping distance. We still aren't sure how Beth managed to bridge the chasm, but we would enter the room to find her perched atop the dresser, preening like a peacock.

One day, with a foot-up on a picnic basket, Beth scaled the kitchen cabinets, using the drawer pulls as footholds. She crawled into the sink and then up into the window sill where she retrieved a bottle of Prell shampoo, which she proceeded to guzzle. Half the bottle was downed before we caught up with her. She blew green bubbles (like Dydee) the rest of the day.

As she grew, one could always spot Beth on the playground. She would be the wiggly form swinging upside down by one leg from the highest monkey bars with dirty smudges on her clothes from shinnying up every pole in the park. Yet she cleaned up like a little lady, with her curly blond hair and her twinkling (with determination) blue eyes.

I tried to take studio-style pictures of Elizabeth in our living room. I'd dress her up and pose her with her stuffed monkey, JoJo, and try to click pictures before she would rebel and refuse to "smile pretty," which was about thirty-five seconds. I loved to show off my sister. Not only was she a beauty, but Mom dressed her like a little princess.

But then boys came into my focus, and Elizabeth became sibling baggage. Now I understood how my brother felt when he was strapped with me. So, without realizing I was following in Don's footsteps, I found a way to leave home. I married.

Elizabeth was the flower girl at my wedding. She was not yet four years old but was resolute in her opinions. During the service, when the pastor was praying, I looked down, and Beth had set her basket on the floor and was removing her dainty white gloves. I signaled with my hand for Beth to pick up her basket, which she responded to with a piercing, "I don't want to!"

I closed my eyes tight and hoped one of us would disappear. When I had no choice but to open my eyes after the pastor's "amen," I found that one of us had. Beth had vanished. All that remained was her abandoned basket and gloves. My flower girl decided she preferred being a spectator rather than a wedding party participant, and she had taken a seat in the front row where she stayed until the service was over.

Elizabeth dilly-dallied through high school until her senior year, when suddenly she cared about her grades and made an all-out effort to do well. And well she did. She not only was an honor student, but Beth also completed more paces (levels of study) in one year than anyone in the history of the school. I have always admired my sister's encyclopedic intellect and her diverse abilities. Elizabeth taught herself to play the twelve-string guitar, she has a lovely singing voice, and she's a wonderful artist.

Today Elizabeth is forty-five and remains resolute in her temperament, and believe me, it's a good thing. Her life has been filled with physical and emotional challenges that she has overcome by God's grace and her grit.

She has homeschooled all three of her children—Steven, Nicholas, and Lindsey—and has cared for our Alzheimer's mom for the past six years. During that time her husband, Bryan, was sent overseas by the Air Force for a tour of duty, and she was diagnosed with breast cancer. The Air Force brought him home while she had her mastectomy but then sent him back to Korea. When Elizabeth had to go through chemotherapy, Bryan was brought home again, this time for good.

While the cancer threat was a major obstacle for Elizabeth, it wasn't the first time her life was in jeopardy. Years prior I picked up the phone to hear a frail voice say, "Patsy."

"Yes, who is this?"

"Elizabeth."

"What's the matter? Are you sick?" I was surprised at how feeble she sounded.

"Yes, I'm very ill, but I don't know what's wrong. I called Bryan, and he's coming home to take me to the doctor, but I felt like I should tell you." (Bryan was stationed in Utah at the time with Elizabeth and the children.)

"Elizabeth, I'm so sorry. You rest, and I'll pray. Let me know what the doctor tells you."

The next phone call I received three hours later was from Bryan. "Patsy, I don't know how to tell you this, but Elizabeth was so bad I took her right to the hospital where they admitted her. The nurse helped her into bed, and Elizabeth went into a coma. She can't hear us when we speak to her. I tried, and so did the kids, but she isn't responding."

Then Bryan said something that confused me. "Patsy, I think if you were here, she could hear you."

I initially tossed away the comment as Bryan's response to stress because I knew, if Elizabeth couldn't hear them, she wouldn't be able to hear me either. I was stunned to think my sister was in a mysterious coma.

Suddenly our brother's death swept over me, and I was deeply afraid. I thought I couldn't go through the loss of another sibling. I remember crying out, "Lord, I never wanted to be an only child. Elizabeth has three young children who need her. Please let her live." But I remembered passionately praying for my brother the same way, yet Don had died; so I knew it wasn't up to me.

The next phone call that came from Bryan was several hours later, and he told me that the doctors still had no idea what was happening to Elizabeth. He recommended that the family gather because it didn't look as if she would survive. Then he repeated, "Patsy, I just feel as though, if you came, Elizabeth would hear your voice."

Numb, I hung up the phone and told Les what Bryan had said. Les responded, "Well, Patsy, God does use our voices at times to speak to others."

The way Les said that made me think of all the times God had used others to speak truth and life into me. I rose up and dragged my suitcase out and began to pack, feeling that, if we were dependent on my voice, we were in a pretty desperate place.

The next morning Les and I were on a flight to Salt Lake City. When we arrived at the hospital, I excused myself before I entered Elizabeth's room, and I stepped inside the bathroom to compose myself through prayer. I remembered how shocking Don had looked when I first saw him in his coma, but I wasn't taking into account that Don had been in a car crash while Elizabeth hadn't.

When I entered her room, she looked like a sleeping child. Why, I thought we could just wake her up and take her home, but of course, she didn't respond.

For days we sat at her bedside, watching the machines and monitoring her every breath. On day five I was seated at her side and was telling her stories from her childhood. My voice seemed to rattle around the room and fall on my own ears.

I said, "I remember the time, when you were three, that you gave your stuffed monkey, JoJo, a sloshing bath in the toilet and then decided you should dry him out in the clothes dryer. Afraid JoJo might get lonesome tumbling around by himself, you threw in Mom's poodle, Sassy, to keep JoJo company. Fortunately, Sassy's whining shrieks alerted the household that he was in a heated situation, and a rescue crew shot into action. Sassy and JoJo survived their tumble, but I must say, Sassy never looked so fluffy."

My eyes were flitting around the room as I talked, and I noticed that Elizabeth's eyes were also flitting around under her closed eyelids, an action we hadn't seen before. So I stood over her and pleaded, "Elizabeth, if you can hear me, I need to know. If you hear my words, open your eyes."

Elizabeth opened her eyes. It took my breath away. I could tell she wasn't focusing, and it didn't appear she could see, but Elizabeth had heard and responded to my request. I bolted for the door to find the nurse, who was walking toward the room as I slid into the hall.

"My sister, my sister opened her eyes on command!" I rattled at her.

The nurse looked at me and calmly stated, "No, she did not."

Stopped in my steps and stumped by her response, I repeated myself, thinking she must not have heard me correctly. The nurse stated, "I know you want that to be true, but I've been working with your sister for nine hours, and she is incapable of responding. Families tend to want responses from their loved ones so much that they imagine things that aren't really happening."

Agitated, I assured her that what I saw had actually happened. To my amazement, the nurse turned and walked into another room. I stepped back into Elizabeth's room and sat next to her, stroking her hand and questioning my own experience. Then the nurse walked in the room and began to adjust surrounding equipment.

I jumped to my feet, and with a strong voice, I said to Elizabeth, "Honey, this is your sister speaking, and I need you to leave your resting place, draw up all your strength, and open your eyes, and keep them open as long as you can, and I need you to do it now!"

The nurse casually looked over her shoulder toward my comatose sister who had stretched open her eyes and was holding them open. The nurse flinched like she had just seen Lazarus. In fact, she almost dropped the IV bag in her attempt to sprint from the room to notify the doctors. In minutes she was back, testing Elizabeth's vital signs. Soon teams of doctors were scurrying around, stunned and suspicious of the reported reversal.

By the following morning, when I walked in, a group of doctors surrounded Elizabeth's bed staring at her as she lay motionless, her eyes closed. They said that I could approach her, which I did. When I called her by name, she almost leapt into my arms. We were all astounded by the sudden thrust of energy she exerted, and then we realized that not only had she opened her eyes but also her eyes were focused, and she recognized me. Elizabeth flailed wildly in an attempt to free herself from the unnatural life-support equipment, not understanding where she was or why she was there.

For me, her strong responses were both thrilling and frightening. I was so relieved to know she was waking up, yet I was concerned that in her panic she would pull all her equipment loose and threaten her progress.

Elizabeth's recovery was miraculous. When she was finally free of her life-support equipment, we asked her what she remembered. She said, "The only thing I remember is the sound of Patsy's voice, and she was talking to me as if I were a child."

"Oh, Elizabeth, did that hurt your feelings?" I asked, remembering the JoJo saga that I had been chattering about when she responded.

"Oh no," she replied. "It was deeply comforting."

I will never know why God chose to use my voice to call

Elizabeth out of her deep sleep, but I will always be grateful. It's like God placed in Bryan's mind the thought that Elizabeth would hear my voice, God gave Les the right words to help me hear past my fear, and God gave Beth an ear to hear her sister's plea. The hopeless situation was reversed through the voices. We never know what God will use, do we? Hope is multilingual.

Elizabeth once asked me, "Patsy, have you ever noticed that we don't relate like sisters?"

"What do you mean?" I responded.

"Well, it's more like you think you're my mom."

"You mean I'm not?" I half giggled. A picture of Beth replacing my Dydee doll flashed through my head.

Hope is multilingual.

6

A Dollar Down, a Dollar a Year

I COULD COUNT ON IT LIKE CLOCKWORK. Every April 3 a song would arrive in my mailbox in the form of a birthday card from my Mamaw (my dad's mother). Inside the card would be a crisp dollar bill. It might as well have been a hundred dollars—it was that important to me. And even though my grandmother was not much on children—until they reached an age at which they obeyed on command, that is—she was big on exchanging mail.

I still have the card she sent me when I turned eight, and I still love it. The card depicts a blond-haired girl holding a woven basketful of kittens. This wasn't one of Mamaw's usual, out-of-the-box cards, but one she had bought from a store display.

That dollar-down-and-a-dollar-a-year investment was about the extent of Mamaw's involvement in my life except for the short visits with her during our vacations to Kentucky and the two times she wintered with us in Michigan.

Still, some of the most soothing sounds during our family's Kentucky vacations were created by the serenade of her home. Summer mornings in the South often turned into sultry afternoons, causing the pace of our days to slow dramatically. Family members would sit on Mamaw's shaded porch with tall drafts of iced tea, while others of us would doze inside.

I loved to nap on Mamaw's generous featherbed, spread across her aging mattress. There I would dreamily listen in on summer as ice rattled against frosty tumblers, rocking chairs moaned from the strain of guests, and buzzing bees tended to the clover outside the open windows. A small table fan whirred sweet relief while stirring the lace curtains in swishing patterns against the peeling wallpaper. Interspersed in this summer symphony was the melody of the creaking screen door, as folks would amble in and out for additional refreshments.

Lulled by the safe sounds of family, I would dangle in that delicate space between awake and asleep, every cell of my being at ease. Then, ever so gently, I would drift off, cradled in a languid lullaby. There's something about napping in your grandma's house that's almost sacred, and even though I didn't go there often, it is still one of my favorite childhood memories.

I also loved Mamaw's homemade peach jam; her hand-woven, multicolored potholders; the fresh-picked tomatoes ripening on her window sill; the smell of yesterdays inside her trunk; and the dear bouquets of lilies of the valley tucked inside water glasses on the rickety wooden table.

My grandmother, whose name was Thanie Elizabeth McEuen, was four years old when Sitting Bull died. Had she been older, I'm sure she would have made him stand. She was thirteen at the turn of the twentieth century, and from that platform she watched (she wasn't much on active participation) the world change. Mamaw witnessed transportation's evolution from her horse-and-buggy days, to Model Ts, to the Wright brothers' airplane, to jets, to a man on the moon. Through her lifetime she stored her food underground to keep it cool; had an icebox for many years; and with much coaxing, reluctantly agreed to a handy-dandy, plug-in-the-wall refrigerator. At the beginning of her life, milk cost seventeen cents a gallon and a loaf of bread was two cents. Grover Cleveland was president when my grandmother was born, and Ronald Reagan was in office when she passed away. Mamaw's life spanned nine decades, and she was a squeak and a feather away from becoming a centenarian, when she died at the age of ninety-seven and one-half.

She was a strait-laced, churchgoing kind of gal who loved the Lord, her family, and the correct way of doing things. In her ninety-seven-plus years, she never donned a pair of slacks; it just wasn't acceptable in her mind. I tried to convince her that during the winter, when she suffered from the cold, it would be okay to slip a pair on under her dress to keep her frail legs warm, but she wouldn't hear of it. And as long as I knew her, Mamaw wore fat-heeled, black, lace-up shoes. She never varied. She loved rules, and she had a ton of them.

"Mamaw" isn't an unusual name for a grandparent, especially in the South, but mine chose it because she didn't like the old sound of "grandmother." She did grandmotherly things with me, though, in the few times we were together. For instance, she taught me the "Now I lay me down to sleep" prayer and how to sign the alphabet for the deaf. I thought those both worthy additions to my life, but she taught me much more without even realizing it.

For example, as a preteen, once I traveled with Mamaw on a Greyhound bus from Michigan to Kentucky. A couple of hours into the trip a youngster accidentally locked himself in the bathroom and was howling out of fear. His mom was having no luck in coaxing him out of his prison; so I rose up to see if I could help. My grandmother gained a firm grip on my arm and pulled me back into my seat. In her mind, we had not been properly introduced to the family, and it would, therefore, be inappropriate to interfere. Mamaw was a very private and cautious woman.

Eventually the child made it out of the back of the bus, but I continued to puzzle over what appeared to be Mamaw's lack of compassion. Years later I realized that Mamaw was afraid—of so many things. And in this, I would mimic her.

Now that I think about it, Mamaw's arrow-straight posture reminds me of someone trying very hard to hold herself together. Mamaw was an orderly lady both in her appearance and her environment. She had very little but kept it clean and in place.

It was as though she believed, if she let down even for a moment, she would permanently unravel.

Her fears probably started to grow because she was a sickly child, suffering from a malady she called "St. Vitus's Dance," which affected her legs. She was sent to live with relatives until she recovered. Mamaw told me her legs were wrapped, and she spent most of her time in bed. Her legs, though spindly, seemed strong enough throughout her adult life, but she seemed to think of herself as feeble. I've wondered, if she had realized she would live almost a hundred years, whether she would have thrown caution to the wind and lived less restrictively.

But Mamaw was satisfied with small pleasures, including growing plants and listening to her favorite inspirational radio shows. With just a tad bit of encouragement, she would conjure up a tune on her harmonica and, with a voice warbled from the years, would sing hymns. I could hear in her voice the hope of glory.

Mamaw was a proper lady through and through. She sat with her feet crossed at the ankles, and her hands and her hankie folded in her lap. She always was courteous; I never heard her say a harsh word to anyone. To tell you the truth, I never heard her raise her voice. She had strong convictions, but she never was deliberately rude. She rose early, tended to her duties, and was in bed by eight . . . on a late night.

Mamaw, conservative even in her faith, told me she was in church one Sunday, and the congregation was singing a series of hymns. She said she felt happy in her heart as she sang, and that at one point in her joy, she leaned her head back with her eyes closed. When she opened them a moment later, the church ceiling had disappeared, and she found herself gazing into Christ's face. She had never experienced anything like that before nor did she again until glory.

I'm so grateful my grandmother shared that experience with me. I've wondered if that type of divine encounter is how Jesus breaks through our rigidity, that we might soften in his holy presence.

Mamaw loved the Lord and loved to attend church. I can still see my grandmother bent over her large-print Bible next to a window, using her bifocals and a magnifying glass in search of the answers for her Sunday school lesson. The Lord was definitely her sustainer.

But one story Mamaw told me helped me to see her faith with fresh eyes. Periodically, after Papaw's death, she would lease out her little dwelling while she rented space in someone else's abode (which never lasted long because Mamaw had tons of opinions that didn't always set well with other folks). On one of those occasions, she saw the Lord provide for her in a special way.

"My renters had moved out," she explained to me, "and I wanted to take a survey of the house. I didn't tell anyone where I was going because I didn't think it was any of their business.

"When I arrived, I walked through each room, looking for any repairs that might have to be made. Then I stepped into the closet to make sure nothing had been left behind, but as I turned around, the door snapped shut behind me. Immediately I remembered the lock I had installed on the closet door at the renters' request, and I grabbed for the knob. Try as I might, I couldn't budge the door. I realized I was trapped inside, and not a soul knew where I was. Suddenly telling someone where I was going seemed wiser."

"Oh, Mamaw, you must have been afraid," I said, imagining how I would feel inside a closed, dark, small space.

"That was when I began to pray," Mamaw said. "I realized no matter how long I wrestled that door, it wasn't going to open. Relinquishment was my only hope."

"Relinquishment?"

"I've been a widow for a long time," she continued, "and I learned early on there would be many situations that would be beyond my control, and I would have to trust God with the outcome."

"What happened?"

"I began to pray aloud, 'Jesus, you are light, and I am in a dark place; you are freedom, and I am a prisoner; and Lord God, I am a widow, and you promised to be my husband. Please send someone to open this door."

Mamaw told me that before she could say, "In the name of Jesus, amen," she heard a loud snap, which caused her head to pop up, and her eyes to open. She saw a shaft of light and realized the door was ajar.

"I knew he would answer me, but quite honestly, I didn't think he'd do it that quick," Mamaw said. "I didn't know who he had sent, but I couldn't wait to thank them. I stepped out of the closet, but no one was there. 'Howdy, Howdy,' I called as I made my way through the house.

"Finally," she said, "I was in the front yard still calling, 'Howdy,' when it hit me: The Lord himself had set me free!"

Yes, Mamaw believed in and had experienced God's hand in her life many times. Relinquishment isn't easy, especially for tightly structured folks like my grandmother and me. Perhaps that's why closet experiences are almost a necessity for us, if we are ever to experience liberty at the level of our spirits.

Still, Mamaw was a mix of faith and fear. She reminds me of the man who came to Jesus and said, "I believe, help thou my unbelief." Examining Mamaw's life has helped me to see my own contradictory behavior more clearly. The melding of our humanity and our faith is bound to show forth flaws.

Mamaw also was a mix of demure and dashing. She was extravagant in two areas: her hair and slashes of red clothing. She couldn't bear being gray-headed; so she kept a red rinse on her hair until the day she broke her hip and could no longer get around. And she would adorn herself with scarves, hankies, and hats that were as red as a strawberry.

But the most radical thing my grandmother did in her life was to marry. Her decision was radical not because she married, but because she was twelve years old when she wed Papaw. Nope, that's not a typographical error; she was twelve. Actually, it wasn't as scandalous as it sounds to us today, although even then some eyebrows arched. You see, Papaw was in his twenties. (Twenties? Now my eyebrows are heading north.) Yet even with that age difference, I'm told no one doubted that Mamaw was the main influencer of her and Papaw's daily choices. And I believe it, having had a number of rules set down for me by my starched grandmother.

While Mamaw's personality loomed large, other aspects of her life seem to have shrunk, as I see them through adult eyes. For instance, when as I child I visited Mamaw, she would make oatmeal and serve it in emerald green bowls that she got free out of cereal and detergent boxes. I loved those bowls, so when I grew up, I asked her for one. She sent several. I was amazed at how small they were.

Why, even Mamaw's house seems minuscule to me as I think about it today. Of course, it was small. Counting the addition of a new-fangled flush toilet, her house was about five hundred square feet. That's the size of my storage-laden garage.

As a child, the tree beside her house seemed massive; it leaned over the home as if to protect its small form from harsh winds. Unfortunately, regardless of the tree's efforts, the blustery winds of life and loss blew through Mamaw's abode again and again.

My grandmother buried her husband after fifty years of marriage (she would live more than thirty years alone). She also buried her first child before he was a year old, and because of her long life, she would bury her only daughter, Ada, and both of her other sons, Donald and Waller. Mamaw knew loss, grief, and great sorrow; yet, fearful person though she was, she remained steadfast in her faith.

Hope is ageless.

*D*O YOU REMEMBER BRER RABBIT? If so, you recall that his hope looked, well, hopeless when Brer Fox finally snagged Rabbit by the throat. Fox had waited a long time to wrap his hands around that long-eared, fur-faced varmint, his archenemy. And now that Fox had, he was licking his lips in anticipation of a barbeque, a stew, or maybe french-fried rabbit. Yum. But before the barbeque pit could heat up, Rabbit convinced Fox that for Rabbit, being thrown into the briar patch was a far worse death. Fox, beguiled into believing the patch was Rabbit's worst nightmare, heaved Rabbit headlong into the briars. Thinking his problems were over, Fox was startled back into reality when he heard a song, a song mind you, dance forth from the briar patch . . .

"I was born and raised in a briar patch. Oh, my Lord, He's sure been good to me. I was born and raised in a briar patch!" Brer Rabbit, a pro at doing the bunny hop while dodging briars, was singing a taunting song of victory.

I'll tell you what, I want to break into song myself and click my heels, when I think about the South. It makes me want to sing, "Oh, my Lord, He's sure been good to me, I was born and raised with a Southern heritage!"

Even though I was the first in our family line to be born and raised in the North, I've always had a passion for my Southern roots. I loved that my parents had an "accent" and said, "Y'all come, hear?" Although I must confess I did feel a tad disconnected since the rest of my kin were from Kentucky while my birth certificate proclaimed *Michigan.* I didn't prefer Kentucky over Michigan, but I wanted to be like and talk like "my people." I didn't want to be different than those whom I loved.

That sense of not quite belonging would trail me all my life, nipping at the heels of my self-esteem. In fact, years into my adult life, a counselor had me jot down answers to a series of personal questions, including my two favorite movies. I chose *Anne of Green Gables* and *Heidi.* Noting my choices, she said, "Isn't it interesting that your two favorite movies are both about orphans?" I thought about that and realized, as loving as my parents were, I grew up with a sense of not quite belonging. As a child, I remember planning that, when I grew up, I would move to Madisonville, Kentucky, in hopes of closing the gap in my heart.

Nothing brought the sound of music to my young heart

quicker than my parents announcing we were going to Kentucky for a visit. I loved seeing my grandmother, aunts, and cousins. The smell of green beans simmering on the back burner, the sight of pies cooling on the counter, and the sound of my kin all chattering together tickled my heart.

My mother and her sisters would sit around in rockers with enameled pans full of green beans in their laps. I loved the distinct sound of the beans snapping and the joyous music of the sisters laughing.

As soon as we hit town, we would go straight to Mamaw's house on East Broadway Street. I knew the first thing she would do was take hold of my arm and squeeze it, like one might a tomato, to determine my well-being. It was Mamaw's form of a dipstick to see how I was faring. Mamaw's first comment would be based on whether I felt scrawny or was putting on weight. "Why, Patsy, I believe you've put on some flesh since I saw you last." Or she would say, "Child, you better eat more; you feel plum puny."

Next we would visit my aunts, uncles, and cousins. My aunts were amazing women who could run a business, pluck a chicken, crochet a bedspread, plant a crop, churn butter, play instruments, raise families, and survive hardships with grace and dignity.

If you were in need of a dress for church, you would make your way to Aunt Hazel's farm, and she would measure you up and sew you a new creation that same day. And cook? Oh, my, just gather up my aunts, or select any one of them, and you would have a feast you wouldn't soon forget. My Aunt Elvira could also drive a tractor, paint a picture, or strum her mandolin with the best of them. Aunt Pearl could make you a stitch-perfect quilt, a banana cake to die for, and cause you to giggle yourself silly and then sane again. And the Myers girls were compassionate toward the hurting and the needy.

All my aunts were brief in stature. Hazel was trim, but Elvira and Pearl were a little more roundish with long hair. Elvira wore braids that encircled her head. Pearl wound her hair into a bun on the back of her head and often topped it off with a hair net. And they did so enjoy being together.

Yet, with all the celebrating we would do when our family went south and all the fun we would have, I faced a major obstacle again and again. The dreaded outhouse. I was scared to death of the little wooden building with the bees and yellow jackets that stood guard, buzzing over the two-seater. I hated the smell, the isolation, the spidery knotholes, and the threat that I might fall through or get stung or both. I'd rather have stomachaches than make the long walk out to the creepy, crooked structure and take care of business. Besides, I had heard snakes would slither up and bite your bottom. And once my cousin even saw a black widow spider on the wall. (I bet he said that just to shake up his citified cousin.) If Brer Fox had wanted to end my life, the worst way possible was to lock me in the outhouse. Trust me, you wouldn't have heard music coming forth—a scream, yes, but nary a song. I was grateful when all my kinfolk eventually invested in indoor plumbing.

Out of all my aunts, I'm probably most like Pearl. She loved the Lord, was quick to defend the truth, was a bundle of nervous energy, had a sassy sense of humor, and was not someone you would want to cross. Yep, we had definite similarities. But, of course, we were also different.

For instance, Aunt Pearl was famous for being ready at a moment's notice to go anywhere with anyone who would call on her, be it a friend, a neighbor, or a family member. And she usually didn't announce her departure or her arrival until she was there. Why, one time she called her daughter-in-law Laurie and said, "I've gone on a trip."

"Where you at, Momma?" Laurie asked, puzzled because Pearl sounded so far away.

"Oh, I'm in Germany," she answered. Seems a friend mentioned the evening prior that she wanted to see her grandson, and Pearl said, "Well, let's go," and they were off.

I remember, when I was growing up, that Aunt Pearl would either appear at our door unexpectedly or call in the night, lost in Detroit (fifteen miles from our home), and want my dad to come and lead her to our house.

"Okay, Pearl, I'll come get you," Dad assured her. "But where are you at?"

"Well, I don't know. If I knew, I wouldn't need you to git me. I'm in a phone booth. Let me ask this here policeman."

"Policeman? Pearl, what are the police doing there?" Dad questioned wide-eyed.

"Well, he stopped me fer goin' the wrong way on a

one-way street, but I told him I was only goin' one way. He said he wouldn't give me a ticket, if I'd call someone to help me find my way. So git down here to De-trit and git me."

"De-trit's a big place Pearl," Dad said with a laugh. "I'll need a little more information."

I can't tell you how hard my family would guffaw when Pearl hit town. She truly was a pearl, unique in her ability to bring good cheer. And she was a woman who knew how to pack light. Stuff never encumbered her. That impressed me, the stuff junkie of the world.

My mom told me that, when Pearl's four children were little, it wasn't unusual to hear a tapping on our front door only to discover Pearl and her young'uns standing on the porch. Pearl would be toting a single grocery sack, which contained clothes for the five of them and soda bottles filled with milk and with nipples on them for the babies. With these meager provisions, they would stay a week.

Life at our home took on added dimension and color with Pearl's visits. Why, I could hardly wait to get up in the morning, knowing that every minute she stayed would be an adventure. Even breakfast. Pearl and Mom would team up to fix eggs, bacon, fried potatoes, and baking powder biscuits. Then Pearl would take a tube of store-bought biscuits, shape them into doughnuts, and deep-fry them. Then she would drop the doughnuts in paper sacks full of brown sugar and powered sugar and shake. Oh, my, but they delighted my young palate. Pearl loved to eat, and we loved to join her.

Bedtime was a joy for me when Pearl was there, because I could sleep on a featherbed on the floor. We would shake the pillowed bed until the feathers were thick with air, and then I'd flop down on it, sinking into its downy comfort. To have my Aunt Pearl close by and to sleep on the featherbed—it didn't get any better than that.

All her life my Aunt Pearl traveled light, fast, and unexpectedly. Her death was no exception. Pearl died of a stroke while seated in church praising the Lord. If she had written her own script, that's the way she would have wanted it. One breath she was with us, the next she was with Jesus. And once again Pearl would be remembered for her spur-of-the-moment departure.

Yes, my song of the South would have to contain a verse or two celebrating my aunts, especially Pearl. Her determined stance, her quirky nature, and her passionate faith were an inspiration. She was my feisty aunt, full of spunk and surprises. Pearl also was well acquainted with hard work, great sorrow, and briar patches, which just seemed to enhance her luster. She was one of those gems who, even in memory, keeps refracting light. Hope illuminates even briar patches.

"Oh, my Lord, he's sure been good to me. . . ."

Hope illuminates even briar patches.

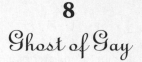

8
Ghost of Gay

I WAS ECSTATIC when my best friend, Carol, invited me to vacation for a week with her family in Michigan's Upper Peninsula. We were both fifteen years old, and Carol and I were to baby-sit her family's little kids, which sounded like more fun then hanging around my house. Besides, the kids weren't so young that they would require much attention.

Carol and I weren't sure my mom would consent. She liked me to be home so I could help with my baby sister. Besides, she didn't know Carol's parents very well, which was good from our vantage point. Carol and I knew that her parents were going for the express purpose of drinking all week, and since my folks didn't approve of drinking, they wouldn't allow me to tag along if they knew the week's agenda. Carol's parents wanted us not only to watch the younger ones while they drank but also to oversee the kids if the adults had hangovers the following morning.

Much to my delight, my parents agreed to let me go. Perhaps a summerful of my pouting didn't appeal to them. Whatever the reason, I was thrilled because, while my mom was full of rules, Carol's mom had very few that would impede us from having a good time. Not that her mom was all fun and games because Gloria had an intimidating anger that scared the stuffing out of Carol and me.

Prior to our departure, Gloria reminded us repeatedly that our destination was practically a ghost town; no boys would be around. Hmm, maybe that's why Mom let me go. The population at our northern destination was barely a hundred people; although once I was there I decided a number of the town folk had expired, and no one had taken a recent tally. It really did seem like a ghost town. Seldom did you see anyone on the streets or even driving around this remote settlement that skirted Lake Superior in the Keweenaw Peninsula. But deer and bear promenaded right through the middle of town, which consisted of a tiny grocery store with two gas pumps, a deserted schoolhouse, a post office in the front room of someone's home, a town hall where a few women wove rugs, a fire vehicle (red Army Jeep with a water tank), one solitary church, and a generous-sized tavern. As you entered the town, a sign proclaimed, "Welcome to Gay." Yep, Gay, Michigan. (When I was growing up, "gay" meant "happy.")

Our first day in Gay was an eyeopener. As we meandered through the town, we decided the homes were odd. They were tall and narrow with high foundations to accommodate the huge snowfalls (an average of 260 inches each winter). Smokestacks on saunas peeked out of backyards, and the most populated spot, the tavern, seemed always to have a few cars parked outside. Besides alcohol the tavern offered smoked herring, chubs, and Finnish pasties (a meat pie, usually made with venison), all of which I had never eaten before.

Carol and I were fascinated with the rugged surroundings but concerned after scoping out the place that her mother was right—there were no boys. But those fears dissipated when, out of nowhere, the ghost of Gay appeared. Actually, he was driving a 1956 Rocket 88 Oldsmobile filled with a cargo of other boys. Little did I realize, when Gloria informed us we would be staying in a ghost town, that I would marry that "ghost."

The reckless apparition behind the wheel, Les, lived in Gay, and the young men in the car were friends he was driving home from football practice. Les thought he was cool, and I thought I was cool; so the third time Les rocketed past us, honking the horn like Clarabel the clown, I stepped into the street to slow him down. Much to my surprise, he accelerated. Clarabel, alias A. J. Foyt, motivated me to retreat to the edge of the road, and then he hit the brakes. When the car stopped, he leaned out the window and bellowed, "What are you trying to do? Get killed?"

"What's it to you? Find another road!" I roared. (Wasn't that romantic?) I then stamped off to the tavern where Carol's family was having lunch.

Shy Carol was appalled that the driver and I had immediately clashed. I mean, what were the chances there would be more boys in this desolate place? But I was indignant. I thought that guy deserved to live in a remote village.

Minutes later Les returned with his friend Joey in tow. Carol convinced me to walk outside the tavern for a minute so she could meet Joey, having noted his winsome face on our previous brief encounter. When I stepped out the door, Les made a few wisecracks to me while I fired back a few of my own. We both had met our match, although I believe Les one-upped me on being outrageous.

After several more encounters, including strolls along Lake Superior, Les and I were in love. Okay, okay in like. Before parting, we agreed to write to each other once I overcame the obstacle of telling my mother I had a boyfriend. I couldn't imagine that she would approve of a boy writing to me, yet I was willing to incur her wrath because I liked Les so much.

Mom actually handled the news better than I thought she would. She rolled her eyes and walked out of the room.

Les was five-feet-nine-inches tall, with dark curly hair, brown eyes, olive skin, and a muscular build acquired from working on fishing boats. It all added up to his being handsome. He had a dreadful mouth full of foul language, a tender heart, and a rowdy sense of humor. I wasn't used to being around such off-color talk, and after a couple of short visits, I told Les that, if he couldn't clean up his language, he didn't need to come around anymore. As he walked away, I figured

I wouldn't see him again, but the following day Les was back, and he made a valiant effort to interact differently.

Over the next two years, Les and I saw each other a total of thirty days, always in the company of others. We got to know each other mostly through exchanging letters and talking on the telephone. Then Les, on a lark, joined the Army and was stationed in Fort Knox, Kentucky. He called me shortly before boot camp was over, and we decided to get married—another lark. I had just turned seventeen and he eighteen.

My mother was both appalled and relieved when I announced our plans. My dad had no reaction. Mom knew I was ill-equipped to handle marriage yet she didn't know what to do with me. I had quit school when I was sixteen and in the eleventh grade. At first I was relieved because I wasn't doing well in my classes and was belligerent toward authority. But by the time Les and I started talking about marriage, I had grown restless and difficult, not knowing what to do with myself.

The only requirement Mom placed on me when I proclaimed that Les and I planned to get married was that the ceremony be conducted in our church. Les was of a different faith, but it wasn't important to him so he didn't mind. My dad loaned us ten dollars, and we bought our wedding bands at the dime store for five dollars each.

Our wedding took place on a pleasant evening, July 14, 1962. The service was brief, and afterward we had our reception in the church basement. Following the reception, a small family group met at my parents' home.

During the course of the evening, my sister-in-law took me aside and told me not to let my brother know where Les and I planned to spend our honeymoon night lest he harass us with phone calls. When she said that, I became very quiet because I hadn't made any plans to stay anywhere. It had never entered my mind.

My parents didn't speak of such things as sex and must have thought I had covered that base. Les wasn't familiar with my home area and must have figured I had somewhere in mind. Not wanting to tell anyone I hadn't a clue where to go and that I hadn't made any reservations, I called for a cab and had the driver take us to the only place I could think of—a small motel I had noticed behind the church we had just married in.

Picture this: I'm in a three-piece knit, going-away suit and gold high heels, with an orchid corsage perched on my jacket. Les is still in the white-jacketed suit and cummerbund he had rented for the wedding. We pull up to a dingy motel. The room was sparse but included a slot for quarters on the bed to jiggle you to sleep, and over the television hung a sign that read, "Turn off by 10 p.m." It was 10:15. And this was our first date alone since we had met. Uh-huh, really. What a beginning. Our relationship was far more like a comic book than a storybook.

Two days later, we headed for Kentucky on a Greyhound bus so Les could finish his training and receive his first assignment. Six weeks later, he was sent to Germany where he would be stationed. We wouldn't see each other for eighteen months. This wasn't the lark I had envisioned.

I wandered around from his family, to mine, to my own apartment during that time. I was emotionally floundering. I didn't have the maturity to settle in one place, find a job, and save money. Instead I kept trying to find a place to belong, but I felt like odd-woman-out wherever I went. I was emotionally and relationally tattered, and I made a series of poor choices.

Les had his own problems. While in Germany he received a stack of Article 15s, a court martial for disrespecting a commissioned officer, for drunk and disorderly conduct, and for using obscene language. He even broke his nose in a fight. But somehow he managed, after his tour of duty, to be released with an honorable discharge.

We were quite a couple. Neither of us was prepared to behave, much less be equipped for marriage or the responsibilities it brought. Les and I talked before he came home about whether we wanted to continue our marriage or go our separate ways. We decided to give our relationship a try. When Les returned from Germany, he was twenty, and I was nineteen.

At first, things went well between us, but then I found myself overtaken with an inexplicable sadness. I was unmotivated and couldn't come to grips with my purpose for being alive. I slept too much (twelve hours a night), smoked too much (two packs a day), drank too much coffee (ten pots a day—uh-huh *pots*), and began to lose weight (down to eighty-seven pounds). My choices kept me wired.

Les was puzzled by my eroding lifestyle, and he was frustrated that I slept so much and accomplished so little around our apartment. Eventually he adjusted his life around my quirky behavior, often picking up the slack in our home.

When I found out I was pregnant, I was elated, as was Les. I gained some of my weight back, and for a while I did better and felt good. Then I started to gain too much weight, and once again I was sleeping too much. By the time I went into labor, I had gained more than thirty pounds, which for a five-foot gal like little me is a lot.

Four days after giving birth to our son, Marty, I left the hospital the same weight as when I checked in. My weight, my unsteady emotions, and my fluctuating hormonal levels kept me anxious. Marty had to be rushed to the hospital twice when he stopped breathing. I unraveled. I became overprotective and developed a fear of losing our baby. Many nights Marty slept on my chest and tummy so I could keep him safe. If he choked, I stopped breathing until he caught his breath. I didn't want to leave him with anyone. I almost drove myself—and everyone else—crazy.

My insecurities increased until even the dailiness of life seemed to overwhelm me. The sink and counters were full of dirty dishes, the laundry hamper was overflowing, and the cupboards were empty. The disarray in the house paralyzed me even more. Often Les, after work, would clean up the kitchen, or run to the Laundromat and grocery store for us.

Les tried to be understanding, but my fears were often so

illogical that it kept our home and relationship off kilter. My fear of storms had grown to such proportions that even a gust of wind would send me searching for cover.

I remember Les talking me into spending a night in a friend's pop-up camper at a campground ten minutes' drive from our home. That evening, as we settled in for the night, a storm whipped up. The fellow behind us hadn't fastened his awning poles securely, and when a gust caught the awning, the poles yanked out of the ground and flipped over onto the camper in a great clatter. I was terrified and insisted that Les immediately take me home. By the time we arrived home, the storm cloud had dissipated.

Les had grown up in dysfunction; so while the atmosphere was familiar, the radical behavior of his first family and our home life differed. Les's dad, Lawrence, a lumberjack, was an alcoholic and a dangerous man. His abusive actions often sent his six children scurrying for cover under tables and behind chairs. Les said that frequently his dad's anger was focused on beating Les's mother, Lena. They never knew what would set Lawrence off, but whatever was at hand became his weapon, whether it was a gun, a knife, or a two-by-four. They feared for their safety and the well-being of their mother. Les's mom was a hardworking woman with six children, who was caught in a web of abuse with seemingly no way out. Les absorbed guilt for not being able to rescue his mother, and as an adult, he became very protective of me.

When Les's dad was in his midforties, he decided to stop

drinking, but the sudden withdrawal threw his body into seizures. Les and his brother Fred rushed their dad to the hospital, but, as they carried him into the emergency room, he died in their arms. Les was fifteen.

The death of Les's dad, while a significant loss for the family, was also liberating for them. But Les didn't find freedom an easy thing to handle. At sixteen, he quit school and started a cycle of regular drinking. He worked on a fishing boat on Lake Superior, and the owners were both drinkers. So it wasn't unusual for them all to start off their workday with a breakfast of fish eggs and beer.

The day Les, then eighteen, and two of his buddies signed up for the Army, Les was the only one accepted. He hadn't meant to join up alone, but his name was on the dotted line, and the next thing he knew, he was on a train headed for boot camp. After our marriage, his stint in Germany, and the birth of our first son, Les was faced with yet something else he hadn't counted on, my emotional demise.

After giving birth to Marty, my physical and emotional health frayed even further. Then one day, after a heated conversation, Les turned to walk away, and I had a panic attack. I didn't know what I was experiencing had a name; I only knew I couldn't breathe, and the chaos that created paralyzed me with fear. Les rushed me to the hospital where they gave me an injection to settle me down, but they never told us what was wrong. So I became hypervigilant, fearing that something might trigger my body to once again turn against me. As I grew more and more hesitant to be involved in even normal activities, the friction between Les and me increased as well.

If Les wanted to go to a restaurant in another town, I was opposed. What if a storm came up, what if the traffic was heavy, what if the place was crowded, and what if I didn't feel safe? If we were going with others, I was concerned that they might want to drive, and I could only trust Les to drive. Well, I kind of trusted him.

Les admits he experienced a payoff for putting up with my frenzied behavior: I made him look normal. He became known as the nice guy for enduring me. He looked like a hero, and for me, in many ways he was. But it wasn't that he didn't have his own battles. . . .

Les's drinking became a problem early on in our marriage, and I could see we were headed down a destructive path. Isn't it interesting that I could spot his bad behavior but wasn't dealing with my own? After one particularly unpleasant scene, I dumped his beer down the sink and told him he would have to stop drinking or leave. To my amazement and his, Les never drank again.

But his anger was a far more enduring issue for us. While Les wasn't like his dad, he still was threatening with his anger. He was like a volcano, in that he wasn't riled all the time—in fact, he usually was quite jovial. But he would stuff his feelings until, when he did spew, his lava sizzled over our landscape. While he was never abusive with our children or me,

Les would take his anger out on a door or a wall, which was scary. It would take years for him to learn how to express himself and to manage his anger more acceptably.

What pulled Les out of his anger cycle, after years of trying to live life his way, was inviting Christ into his heart. My life had begun to change (more about that in upcoming chapters), and Les told others that that's what convinced him there had to be a God. Les understood that I didn't have the kind of strength, courage, or fortitude to make the many changes my life needed. He also knew he had his own personal turmoil and needed God to rescue him. Actually, the healthier I became, the more noticeable Les's flaws and brokenness became. While I surely gave Les plenty to be angry about, his main fury stemmed from his violent childhood. I was kindling on already white-hot coals.

Les and I both had to battle our way to a place where we could relate more thoughtfully with each other. But I can't think of a time since I married Les that I haven't loved him, even though I failed him in so many ways. And he would tell you the same about himself. He loved me the best way he knew how. We were wounded, broken, rebellious, willful children when we met, and we have struggled to stay together even when we felt far apart. Jesus has been growing us up in his love, teaching us what it means to love deeply and love well. Many years of relational flailing lapsed before we reached that point. But hope restores confidence.

After Les learned healthier ways to express his anger, qualities that had always been inherent in him began to shine through. He is one of the dearest, most generous men I've ever known. He is tender, funny, romantic, courageous, and caring. He is a great dad (involved and invested) with our sons and an exceptional Poppa to our grandsons.

Les thinks of ways to be thoughtful that never would occur to the rest of our family. For example, after my dad died, my mom experienced a great gap in her life. Les saw her pain and wanted to ease her loss. So each Christmas he made certain she received a box of chocolate-covered cherries, the gift Dad had always given her.

I, too, have been a recipient of his generosity. Months before his open heart surgery, Les picked me up from the airport and wanted to take me to a fine hotel for dinner. I objected. I wasn't in the mood for fancy. He asked where I wanted to go, and I answered, "Bob Evans." I could tell that didn't appeal to him, but he took me there anyway.

Once we were seated, he pulled out a ring box and said, "This just doesn't seem like a Bob Evans kind of moment, but here goes." He went on to say that, with his heart surgery coming up before our twenty-fifth wedding anniversary, he was concerned that, if he didn't pull through the operation, he might leave me without having ever given me a diamond.

After his little speech, Les opened the box to reveal a ring with a cluster of small diamonds—twenty-five of them, one sparkling reminder for each year we had been married. Even over my plateful of waffles, I was once again smitten with the ghost of Gay.

Hope restores confidence.

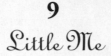

9
Little Me

*I*T'S NOT EASY WATCHING ONE'S LIFE SHRINK to the thousand square feet of one's home. But when my life reduced down to my six-by-four-foot mattress, I knew I was in big trouble.

The morning I awoke and realized my world was the size of my Sealy Posturepedic because I didn't want to get up anymore, the question ran through my mind, *Patsy, where will you go from here? The bathtub? Down the drain? The loony bin?*

I had plummeted deeper and deeper into my fears. I was afraid of driving; riding in cars; storms; being alone; being in large groups; taking medications; not taking medications; driving over bridges, through tunnels, up mountains; stepping into elevators; dealing with heights; and other people's opinions.

Why, I even feared grocery stores. No, not the broccoli, silly, but the aisles. They had begun to close in on me. All the different choices made me dizzy, disoriented, and anxious. So you can imagine, with my expansive fears, how complicated and narrow my existence had become. I had no idea that my struggles were a condition that others suffered from and actually had a name: agoraphobia. All I knew was that my fears culminated in my being unable to leave home and then, eventually, scared to get out of bed.

Morning was difficult for me. My limbs felt heavy and my thoughts dark. I had trouble leaving the shelter of sleep and facing myself. Even the simplest of tasks seemed overwhelming—bathing, fixing my hair, washing the dishes, cooking, and cleaning. A prevailing sadness stalked me, and my self-loathing was debilitating. I even felt sorry for the hair stylist, who had to look at me while she cut my hair.

My days were a blur of tedium. Most hours felt centuries long. I accomplished little and anguished much with anxiety crouching in every corner of the house. I tried to escape through television movies, but mostly I paced the floor or sat, doing nothing but worrying. And, of course, trying to drown my fears in cup after cup of coffee while I popped my tranquilizers. Listening to radio weather reports and watching potential storm formation out my window occupied me as well. At night I begged God, through waterfalls of tears, to rescue me from the scary pit I was in.

I felt as if I were caught in a mental and emotional whirlpool of anger, fear, guilt, shame, and melancholy. And while I despised my condition, I despised myself even more.

I was failing in my life roles; yet I fought tenaciously to defend myself and my behavior. Then I would spiral deeper into self-pity. I didn't seem to have the skills or the wherewithal to pull out of my sick cycles.

This was my life in my late teens and early twenties. After five years of increasingly neurotic behavior, because the situation looked hopeless, I cast myself on my physician, begging him to help me find a way out. I was twenty-three years old.

My doctor's eyes sent a clear message: He didn't hold out much hope for me. He had watched my descent; he could see how stuck I was. I was taking four strong tranquilizers a day, which caused him to remark, "I give you enough to knock out a horse, and it barely fazes you."

I was making regular trips into the emergency room for shots of Demerol when I was overtaken with anxiety. I didn't understand I was experiencing panic attacks. I thought I was dying or, scarier yet, losing my mind.

My doctor had hospitalized me on several occasions when I was a tight knot of nerves. He used those times to run tests and give me an opportunity to rest, hoping that would help me to gain a better grip. When I finally hit bottom though, and begged him to help me, he recommended a self-help, mental health group called Recovery, Inc., which held meetings twice a week in my area.

The very week he told me about the group, I attended my first meeting. I asked Les to come with me and wait outside in case I became too uncomfortable or too afraid. That way I would know I had a way of escape. I remember feeling apprehensive on the ride to the meeting and making Les promise over and over that he would wait for me.

I think my bewildered husband realized that without a breakthrough our future and the future of our three-year-old son, Marty, was bleak. Neither of us knew for sure what Recovery meetings were, but we both, in an unspoken agreement, decided to chance it. This meeting felt like my last hope.

Hope comes as a companion; she slips her arm around your shoulder and offers to help you stumble toward change. That evening, while Les waited outside, I heard hope whisper, "You are not alone." And then, as if to visually underscore that thought, I found myself seated at a large table in the basement of a big church with a small crowd of anxious people. I sat on the edge of my chair, my heart pounding with anticipation, and drank in every word that was spoken. It was as if, for years, in my attempts to explain my inner turmoil, I had been speaking Yiddish to folks who only spoke English. Now I was encircled with those who spoke my language and who had a heart for my plight. I felt understood by these people who were strangers when I walked in and kindred souls by the time I walked out.

Sometimes hope appears as one bread crumb after another, but suddenly you realize that a crumb of hope is all you need to take the next step and the next step and the next . . . That was what happened to me that night; I spied a bread crumb.

After the first meeting, I never again was taken to an emergency room or admitted into a hospital so I could get a grip. And each time I visited my doctor, instead of looking at me with eyes of pity, he looked genuinely amazed. He would call in any nurse in the vicinity and say, "See her? She's a miracle."

The meetings didn't cure me, but the truth I learned there fanned the embers of my faith, causing hope to flicker. Recovery had guidelines for table discussions that included a list of no-nos. We weren't allowed to talk about age, politics, or religion. And while the insights of Recovery weren't taken out of a church doctrinal statement, I found that they aligned with the Scriptures. Recovery taught about selecting healthy thoughts and not dwelling on fearful or angry thoughts, which only stirred up negative emotional reactions. Scripture puts it this way, "Whatever is true, whatever is noble, whatever is right, whatever is pure, whatever is lovely, whatever is admirable—if anything is excellent or praiseworthy—think about such things" (Philippians 4:8 NIV). And in Corinthians it tells us to cast down imaginations (2 Corinthians 10:5 KJV).

My fears often bullied me around, insinuating that I had no value and that others didn't like me. I had to repeatedly refuse those thoughts and replace them with a healthier way of thinking. In other words, just as we throw out our garbage, we need to cast out thoughts that are trashy.

So while Recovery wasn't a Christian group per se, it wasn't in conflict with my faith, which was important to me since I had received Christ at age twenty, when Marty was born. I already was in emotional trouble by then, but after inviting Christ into my life, I sat down and waited for him to repair me, banish my fears, and release me from the stranglehold of guilt and shame. I thought he would slip in while I was sleeping and wave away my brokenness so I could arise into a new day with a full heart of hope. But it wasn't happening. I didn't give up my faith. I just figured God didn't think I was worth his time, and I didn't blame him.

I've found that we fearful people often deny ourselves entry through the doors that lead us to healing and growth. We cower lest we make one more mistake or open ourselves up to something that will cause our demise. So we hunker down in our pain and terror and attempt to survive our self-imposed isolation. We cry out that we want to be different, yet we refuse to budge from our atrophied existence.

Fortunately for me, after only a few Recovery meetings, I was able to follow hope's breadcrumbs back to church. It was one of my first social outings aside from trips to the doctor's office and the meetings. The church was small, with just a handful of parishioners, but it was a major step forward for me. For years, the thought of being in a sanctuary and having a panic episode was too disconcerting to consider. Now, though, I had some tried-and-true mental tools. If my emotions betrayed me with a flurry of suggested dangers, I could manage.

Since Les, who was twenty-five years old at the time, had recently decided to follow Christ, we became a team committed to that small church family. Our pastor, Don Kirkland, and his wife, Norma, developed into dear friends, and under their tutelage Les and I began the slow process of growing in our faith.

In Recovery I learned that I could make my muscles mind by commanding them to do the very thing they didn't want to do. In other words, I needed to develop discipline. I had been told I needed discipline before, but Recovery taught me how to experience success, and when I did fail, how to begin anew.

I started with simple tasks, which I've since learned are sacred tasks because they are the building blocks that prepare us for the tough stuff of life. I remember for a while I made pies. Every day I baked pies as part of my personal therapy. We had so many of them, we would give them to anyone who would stop by, even the mail carrier. I also made my bed every day, fixed my hair, applied my makeup, and washed the dishes.

The result of being faithful in these small things was the restoration of my sense of worth and dignity. And proper placement restores order to one's surroundings, which in turn restores order to some of the brain's clutter.

Don't misunderstand; I'm not suggesting that if our homes are tidy, our emotional health is guaranteed. Yet for many, restoring order is a first important step, and I was one of those.

I was faithful to attend the Recovery meetings twice a week for one year. The Lord continues to use what I learned at those gatherings to help me maintain good mental health.

One of the takeaways that continues to benefit me is the truth that emotions don't always give accurate information. Or, as my friend Marilyn Meberg puts it, "Emotions don't have brains." God designed emotions to feel and brains to reason. For years I had bought into the erratic information my emotions were screaming as if it were gospel. My emotions convinced me I wasn't safe or sane.

I gradually came to a point where I realized I couldn't rely on my emotions as my life gauge. And with that understanding, hope sparked the possibility I could become more functional, maybe even normal. However, I've given up on normal as a life-goal, having realized that "normal" is just a setting on one's dryer.

Even after Recovery laid the groundwork for my personal recovery, I had many difficult choices ahead of me, and God had several surprises lying in wait as well. In my mind, I was still Little Me in a very big, scary world.

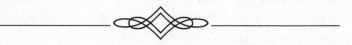

Hope comes as a companion; she slips her arm around your shoulder and offers to help you stumble toward change.

10

Venturing Out

LIKE A BANNER waving over my life was the theme "Overwhelmed." It didn't take a lot to tip my scales and with as many hang-ups as I had, it was going to take time to overcome them. Not to mention courage.

At Recovery I learned the importance of breaking down my activities into "part acts" so I could manage them. When I awoke in the morning and felt emotionally undone by the day's demands, I would tell myself that I just needed to do the next thing. So I would brush my teeth. Wash my face. Comb my hair. Slip into my jeans and sweatshirt. Then I would give myself credit for all I had done. While it may not seem like much to celebrate, I already had accomplished more than on prior days.

Then, instead of thinking I had to clean the whole house, I would encourage myself to make the bed. With that done, I would rinse the dishes and open the shades. After cheering for my achievements, I would eventually even wash the dishes. Maybe. But if I didn't, I still recognized I was inching forward.

Step by step I worked hard to do what most folks do without thinking. Eventually those tasks grew less taxing and more natural to include in my daily rounds.

When I was a youngster, my mother often did for me what I should have done for myself. She meant it for love, but instead, in some ways, it crippled me. Mom was demanding with certain chores and set impossible standards for them, but in practical matters she covered my bases for me. I didn't pick up my own clothes, make my bed, or know how to run the washing machine. I was lost in the kitchen, useless with an iron, and hopeless with a needle and thread. I don't blame my mom for my young-adult condition because my brokenness was more complex than that. I'm just saying that, when we help our children to become competent, we better prepare them for life.

Once I learned how to be diligent with my daily tasks, I then faced fears like riding in cars. I was a clenched-fist rider, so I practiced relaxation techniques to keep my tension from getting ahead of me. Otherwise, by the time I arrived at my destination, I was a knot of nerves. It took time and practice. I was jubilant when I succeeded, but I tended to beat myself up when I failed. So I had to work on personal forgiveness. Lowering my expectations for my performance helped because I was such a mental perfectionist.

My storm phobia improved when I set limits on how

many times in a day I could listen to weather reports. I memorized verses about the Lord's being our shelter, our refuge, and our hiding place. Part of my struggle was that I feared God was out to punish me and that he would snuff out my life in the fury of a storm. There's nothing scarier than to feel you're on your own and your life is in jeopardy. So my perception of God and his love was askew and needed alignment with the Scriptures and within my quaking heart.

I slowly ventured out and started to drive again. For quite awhile I avoided lefthand turns. I worried that the people behind me would be angry that it took me so long or that I'd pull out too quickly and cause an accident.

Just try driving to a destination and not make any lefthand turns. Trust me, it slows your progress. Eventually I risked the turns until I finally became comfortable with them. My big celebration came when Little Me drove my mom and her sister more than five hundred miles to Kentucky.

Gradually I found myself in situations that allowed me to face my fears of elevators, airplanes, and traversing mountains. At one time I found it intimidating to stay in a hotel above the fifth floor; now it's not unusual for me to be on the twenty-fifth floor. I don't prefer it, but I don't avoid it. Also, I'd rather fly in a full-sized jet, but it's not unusual for me to ride in the little wind-up jobs to get to some locations.

A fear is nothing more than a tangle of feelings. But when those feelings determine the choices we make, they can become full-blown phobias. I know; I collected them like some folks do old coins.

People issues have been a biggie for me. I give new flair to the term *codependent*. I worry about what folks think of me. I've come a long way, but I confess I have had to work hard not to be disconcerted when someone is displeased with me. I anticipate that I won't do everything correctly; yet I worry whether others will have room in their hearts for my failure.

Recently I was giving the initial greeting to the audience at a Women of Faith conference. The audience was especially receptive and in a good mood. The laughter increased my enthusiasm as I bounced around the stage with vigor like I thought I was Winnie the Pooh's friend Tigger. It turned out that I looked like it because dangling out the back of my jacket was a glittering tail. Seems in my haste to dress I had forgotten to fasten my sequin-covered knit belt, and when I stood to talk, it emerged out of my coat and hung and swung behind me as I bebopped from one side of the stage to another.

It's bad enough to embarrass yourself in front of friends much less in front of thousands of newcomers to your life. But then I decided everyone has something trailing her in her life; so when I took the microphone again to introduce the next guest, I swung my glitzy belt over my head to let everyone know I had found my dangling participle. They roared. Gratefully, I've lived long enough to know that if I can own my failures, others won't struggle with them either. So while

I love others' acceptance, I need to accept myself at my dazzling worst or my humbled best.

I've noted through the years that setbacks in our growth will occur. Understanding that became a safety net for me because my tendency, when I would fall back into poor habits or behavior, was to bury myself in guilt. Then I would believe I would always be stuck. I'd never be well. I'd always be a disappointment to God, others, and myself. What helped me to move past my setbacks was recognizing the frailty of the human condition. We will always struggle with something. I needed to forgive myself (the hardest one for me to let off the hook) and not to indulge myself in pity. Pity is no party. Trust me.

Pulling out of me has been some of the healthiest and most liberating steps I've taken. My life had become too much about me. How was I feeling? What made me comfortable? Did I feel safe? My constant introspection kept me in knots and caused me to be self-serving. While it's good to take care of one's self, too much of anything becomes nauseating.

So I began to find ways to serve my family. At first I did spontaneous favors like serving Les coffee, bringing in the newspaper for him, or making bread pudding, which is his favorite dessert. Sometimes I would run him a bath and lay out his clothes as a thoughtful surprise or offer him a head massage or a backrub.

I concentrated on spending time with Marty, doing things he loved. One of his passions was putting together hundred-piece puzzles. So he and I would have contests to see who could assemble his or her puzzle first. Then we would celebrate the winner with bowls of buttered popcorn.

At Christmas Les, Marty, and I would pack boxes in our home for Salvation Army families and deliver them on Christmas Eve. It was our way of stepping out of our meager situation to think of others, who were having even tougher times. I found the simplest of acts could help me get my mind off of myself while improving my relationships with others.

To strengthen my interaction with folks, I had to learn healthier ways of dealing with my exceedingly short wick. Les wasn't the only person in our home with a temper. I began to realize my regular flareups had little to do with the person I was interacting with, but a great deal to do with me. I needed to take verbal responsibility for my behavior. I needed to say, "I'm sorry. Would you forgive me?" I needed to spot and put a name to what I was truly feeling (intimidation, insecurity, rejection), so I didn't use anger as a refuge from my hurt. I needed to ask the Lord to heal my ruptured heart. And I needed to learn more acceptable ways to express my anger so I didn't leave folks whiplashed. That meant learning to speak the truth in love.

As you can imagine, these adjustments took time. Sometimes I did it right, but sometimes I really messed up. Gradually I chalked up more victories than failures.

Learning to establish boundaries in relationships added to my success. I was always stepping over appropriate lines with others, and I allowed folks to ride roughshod over me. I was not good at saying the word no, nor did I readily acknowledge the noes of others.

Les and I struggled with changing the ways we behaved with each other because we were such a constant in each other's lives and we were so entrenched in our codependant behavior. In fact, at first, when we would change a habit, like not entering into the other person's bad day, it felt like desertion, as though we were saying, "I don't care enough about you to notice you're struggling or to join you in your misery." But as we worked on individualizing, we loved the freedom it brought to our hearts as well as our relationship. One thing that helped as we pulled apart so we could reunite in healthier ways, was to reassure each other that, even though we were making changes, we still loved each other. The adjustments weren't about our loss of love but about our increase in maturity.

We all have emotional hot buttons, and one of mine was abandonment. Les figured that out early in our marriage; so, whenever we had a big fuss and he felt like he wasn't winning, he would threaten to leave. That would do me in every time, and I would quickly retreat into regret. So Les's threats became an effective way to control me.

After years of living under that weight, I realized it wasn't healthy for either one of us, nor was it kind. So one day, after we had recovered from a squabble, I sat down with Les and laid out our reactionary pattern: We would bicker, he would threaten, and I would retreat. Nothing was resolved, neither of us changed, and we not only were stuck like a car in a snowbank, but I also lived in dread that he would abandon me. Then, in love, I told Les that the next time he felt he needed to leave me, he should go. No threats, no manipulation, no intimidation, just take his things and leave. Did I want him to go? Of course not, but I had reached a point where that had become a better option than to continue with our crippling behavior. I'm thankful that he agreed our pattern wasn't a loving resolution to our spats.

Likewise Les had to call me into accountability regarding my part in our spat dilemma. I had always been quick with words and able to twist things around to my favor. This disturbed Les who, while quick-witted, wasn't as fast at expressing his emotions verbally. He couldn't keep up with my flurry of accusations and demands, which left him exhausted and frustrated. And because I didn't know when to withdraw and let him catch his breath, he would reach into the bottom of his argument arsenal and pull up his threat to leave.

In my family, my parents never argued in front of me; while in Les's home, his father was the only one who had a say, and he was constantly ranting. So we didn't have much role modeling to draw from as we worked through conflicts together and tried to leave each other's dignity intact.

While examining our flaws was painful, the process was important because, once we saw the futility of our established behavior, we could set new boundaries and make much needed changes. I became more selective and loving with my verbiage, and Les never again threatened to leave.

The hardest and most humbling work I've ever done is trying to become an emotionally healthy and loving person. It's also been the most necessary, beneficial, and satisfying.

Hope is the harbinger of better things to come.

11
God's Garden

GOD'S SEEDS OF HOPE are often sown by people and books. For me, Rose was used by God to plant a garden of hope in my heart.

I met Rose over the telephone, which seemed prophetic since we would end up spending years of our friendship with phones dangling from our ears, as we conversed about God, husbands, children, and ministry. Rose helped me to start a Bible study in my home and invited me to join her staff at a local women's retreat when I was in my late twenties. Her gentle approach and her spacious, grace-driven heart, offered me a sheltered atmosphere to grow in.

I remember the time Rose prayed God would give me an FM radio so I could listen to her favorite Bible teachers. I thought asking God for a radio was ludicrous. But faith-filled Rose was steadfast in her prayer efforts. Every few days she

would call, and our conversations would unfold something like this:

"Well?" Rose would respond to my "hello."

"Hi, Rose. Well what?"

"Did you get a FM radio yet?"

"No, Rose. And it's not likely to happen, you know. We don't have the money to buy a radio."

"Oh, Patsy, I know that. But God's gonna provide. You'll see; I'll just keep praying."

I'd hang up and roll my eyes. Yeah, right, an FM radio sponsored by God. Uh-huh.

Then one day Les rushed into the house. "Patsy come here; I have a surprise!" I followed him out to a large rental truck. He threw open the door and there, all alone in the cavern, was a long, television console. Some people had given it to Les for helping them out. It was lovely, and I was excited. I called Rose to tell her about it, but I heard disappointment in her voice. "What's wrong?" I asked.

"Oh, I thought you were going to tell me you had an FM radio," she confessed.

I screamed, "Rose, it has an AM-FM radio and stereo! It never hit me; this is God's answer to your prayer!"

Don't ask me how Rose knew God would do that, but she did. After that I wasn't so quick to discard any seeds she wanted to plant in me about God and prayer. I didn't have her mustard-seed faith; mine was more a granule of sand, but I learned to lean on her more mature faith while I was little in mine.

Rose and I were a study in contrasts. Rose was so rose-like, while I was, uh, thornish. She was tall and elegant in appearance while I was short and, uh, prickly. Her gentle disposition and my feisty nature set us up as an interesting combo. Rose's somewhat innocent ways and my jaded perspective kept us approaching life from different angles. She saw the best in everyone while my critical eye caught every flaw. Rose's words were served up with kindness while my off-the-top-of-my-head comments were spicy and, uh, leveling. I needed to be in Rose's friendship circle because she exuded Christ's fragrance.

Once when Rose and I were working on a project at our church, a woman came in and said something very hurtful to me. The jolt of that encounter left me speechless. I made my way into the sanctuary and sat down in a pew to sort out my feelings.

Rose walked by and saw me seated alone; she came in and sat down next to me. "Is something wrong, Patsy?"

I told her what had happened, and I will never forget what Rose did next. She burst into tears. When she caught her breath, she told me how sorry she was that someone would intentionally be cruel to me. I had never had anyone so willingly enter into my pain and literally weep for me. Rose's sincere emotional expression touched me deeply and helped to lift much of the burden I had felt.

Rose willingly planted seeds of grace in the early years of my faith that live in me still. She walked with me on a path toward my healing and celebrated the steps of advancement I made along the way. Rose taught me many lessons by example. Her exuberance for God's Word fanned a flame within me; her tender regard for others exemplified Christ's heart in a tangible way for me; and her willingness to forgive the gravest of offenses taught me about God's mercy.

And Rose cared for me. Once when we went on a retreat, we stayed in a frosty room. Rose loaned me her socks that night so I could sleep while she went sockless. That was Rose.

One day Rose called and invited me to attend a creative teaching class designed to equip teachers, speakers, and writers. Rose and a group of her friends wanted to prepare themselves for ministry and invited me to join them. I decided to tag along because I thought the sound Bible teaching might help me. What never occurred to me was that I would become the star student of the class. It seems God had a plan I would never have thought of, and he decided to spring it on me in a most unexpected way.

Our instructor and Bible teacher, Jill Renich, pulled me aside after she had gone through all of the class's first assignment papers. "Patsy, I'm puzzled by the results of the assignment I gave last week. You seem to be the only one who heard or understood my directions. Do you have any idea why you heard me and no one else did?"

I was stunned. Me, the high school dropout; me, fresh out of my agoraphobia; me, the one who had to pop a tranquilizer to make the thirty-minute ride to attend. Then a possible answer flitted through my mind. "Well, I'm probably the only blank slate in the room. The other ladies all have had quite a bit of schooling, and they may not have as much free space as I do. Everything you say is new to me."

From that point on Jill used my homework assignments as examples for the group. My feet hardly touched the ground. For the first time I could remember, a teacher was affirming me.

At the end of the series, Jill once again took me aside. She had my last paper in her hands and announced that she wanted to send it to *Moody Monthly* magazine along with her recommendation that the editorial staff consider publishing it. I told Jill I'd think about it, but I already knew I wouldn't allow it. My success in her class was the first time since my son's birth that I felt validated, the first time since then that something good had come out of my life, and I couldn't jeopardize it with the threat of a rejection from *Moody*. I went home to live in the joy of Jill's praise. I had no idea that the light of hope that flickered from those classes was the beginning of His unexpected plan for me.

My friends Rose, Joyce, and Mary Ann kept me supplied with Christian reading material to help me in my faith. I read everything I could get my hands on. Our family finances didn't include room for any extras, like books, so I did a lot of borrowing. I became a voracious reader, mostly to help me survive the ongoing mudslide of my emotions and to meet my increased longing to grow in Christ.

I became so passionate about good books that a desire formed in my heart to open a Christian bookstore. The Lord used Rose and Joyce to water that dream with their encouragement and prayers and finally with their financial assistance. I converted a room in my home into "God's Garden of Bibles and Books." Rose and Joyce even had business cards made up for me. I felt so grown-up and legal. To help promote the store's existence, I would pack up boxes of books and take them to churches for ladies events, teas, lunches, and dinners.

God used that seedling of a store to provide not only others with material, but it also kept me with a fresh supply of books to help keep my hope alive. I decided the Lord wanted me to grow up to be a store owner—of course, that was before I found out you actually had to be able to count (I don't do numbers). But once again, he had other plans.

Rose and Joyce had started a neighborhood Bible study that eventually became the base for Women in Action, a ladies' area retreat. They invited me to put a book table in the back of the room on retreat day and sell my materials. I was ecstatic.

But during the program a woman approached the platform and did a five-minute presentation of book reviews. I was mesmerized. She was interesting, funny, and inspiring. I wanted to buy every book she mentioned—and I already owned them. That day a new seed blew into my heart's soil, and I found myself with a growing desire not to just sell books but to tell others about books—books that could change their mind, attitudes, and relationships; books that could nurture their children and inspire their husbands; books that could influence their friends.

For the following Women of Action retreat, the staff invited me to do the "Book Notes," as the book review time was called. I was honored, but the day of the event, when hundreds of women crowded into the room, the honor blossomed into fear. Somehow though, like a robot, I made it to the front of the room, as I heard Rose introduce me. But instead of saying "Patsy Clairmont," she proclaimed, "And now here's Clutzy Paramont." The crowd roared. I stepped onto the stage in a cloud of uproarious laughter, and when the women settled down, I did the reviews.

I think the laughter was my saving grace that day. I was so tight my mainspring would have popped had something not broken the tension, but the women's friendly response to Rose's faux pas helped to spur me ahead. Later the response to my reviews was so positive I became the Women in Action full-time Book Note lady. The Lord would later catapult that "career" into a full-time speaking and writing ministry. It's true, God uses the unlikely.

I'm amazed, as I look back at my progression, how the Lord continually brought just the right person, just the right Scripture, and just the right book when I most needed them. I'm often asked what my favorite books were during my God's Garden years. Well, I especially loved the ones that met me where I was and helped nudge me forward.

One book that remains a constant in my library as well as the libraries of hundreds of thousands of others is *My Utmost for His Highest* by Oswald Chambers. This was my first devotional, and quite honestly, it was over my spiritual head. I didn't get much of it then; yet I would find myself circling back to its rich insights again and again through the years.

Also *Morning and Evening* by Charles Spurgeon remains a favorite. I love his placement of thoughts with their poetic lilt and biblical base.

Hind's Feet on High Places by Hannah Hurnard is an allegory that could be the story of my life. The main character, Much Afraid, is a reluctant journeyer on her way to the high places.

Many of the books I loved then are now out of print, but the one book God used the most to create in me an insatiable hunger for him was the Scriptures. Do I have a favorite book in the Bible? It's difficult to pick. Perhaps Proverbs, James, Philippians, or the Psalms. Of course, I love Genesis, Exodus, and John. Just read them all; it'll do you good! It certainly has me.

Yes, I've watched the Lord press seeds into the sometimes resistant soil of my heart that I might grow out of myself and become more like him. Sometimes he does the planting alone in the night, when it's just him and me. But usually God uses others to plant and water the hope that I can do exceedingly more through Christ than I ever dreamed.

From becoming Book Note Lady at area retreats, I began

to receive invitations to emcee and then later to be the speaker. The transition from book reviewer to speaker took place over about seven years. Every request I received to be a featured speaker was a shock to me. I thought every event would be the last time I would be invited to speak, but the unsolicited invitations kept coming, and I kept showing up. But I had no formal training, and I felt my messages were structurally weak. About that time, I met Florence Littauer, who was a speaker at a conference where I presented the Book Notes. Later, Florence would say that, as I sat on the stage before speaking, I faded into the curtains that served as the backdrop. But when I was introduced, I shot out of my seat like a rocket from a launch pad. And when I opened my mouth, the fireworks started for the audience. Then, after finishing my reviews, I would sit back down and fade into the curtains. Apparently she found some promise in this wallflower, because she invited me to join a training session called CLASS (Christian Leaders and Speakers Services) she was putting together to prepare women for ministry. I attended, and afterward Florence extended an invitation to me to join her on staff to train others. Just like that. She had heard me speak just a few times yet felt I was the right person to work with her. I can only explain her decision as something God put on her heart.

For twelve developmental years, I traveled across the nation with her. Throughout that time, Florence generously invested her years of experience in me. She taught me how to structure a message and how to inject color and interest into my topics. And by example, she demonstrated the importance of stage presence, flexibility, and creativity. She is the most gifted communicator I've ever heard. Florence became my treasured mentor and remains my dear friend.

During those years of traveling and training, one event I spoke at was a women's conference in West Virginia in 1991. Following that weekend, one of the women who had attended sent my taped message to Focus on the Family. I later received a call from Focus asking permission to air my "God Uses Cracked Pots" message on the radio program. After the broadcast, a landslide of invitations from around the nation poured in. Then Focus invited me to write my first book based on the aired message and called it, naturally, *God Uses Cracked Pots*—a dream I never believed could come true. Through Focus I was introduced to my editor, Janet Kobobel Grant, who has nurtured me in my writing and has become a lifelong friend. Who would have believed that I now have thirteen published books and have coauthored ten more with my Women of Faith team members?

Today I travel full-time with Women of Faith and have been with them since their inception, more than eight years ago. Women of Faith has the distinction of being the largest women's conference in our nation; we've spoken to more than 2 million women. Such a privilege is beyond anything I could have imagined. And I've had the delight of working with the core team of Sheila Walsh, Thelma Wells, Marilyn

Meberg, Luci Swindoll, Barbara Johnson, Nichole Johnson, and Mary Graham. Each has become a treasured friend and has added immeasurably to my heart and soul.

Mary Graham, the president of Women of Faith, is one of the most sterling examples of God's strong grace that I've witnessed. Her leadership is a mix of kindness and wisdom lit by Christ's love. Her persistence brought me to the point of writing this book. I thought the task daunting, but for several years Mary gently nudged me until I became willing to try to tell my story. Reviewing my life has been a sweet agony and a powerful reminder that, indeed, "with God all things are possible (Mark 10:27 NKJV)." Mary served as the catalyst for me to remember afresh that the Lord is God of all hope.

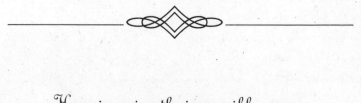

Hope is seeing the impossible emerge
out of a broken life.

12

Coconuts and Chocolate Pop

FIRSTBORNS SHOULD BE DISPOSABLE—for their own protection." I don't know who first dared utter that thought, but it holds a lot of truth. We practice on firstborns, as we struggle to figure out parenthood, only to realize twenty years later there possibly was a better way to do it.

Last week I bought my husband a twenty-inch television set for Father's Day. It came in a big box with a book of instructions almost as voluminous as the container. When I gave birth to our nineteen-inch firstborn, all I was handed was a voluminous bill and instructions to sit on a pillow for a few weeks. No operating manuals, no spare parts, and no guarantees came with this intricate creation.

I remember that my pregnancy felt eternal. Within weeks of finding out I was expecting, I inflated like a blow-up chair. After gaining thirty pounds, I waddled my way through to delivery. Even the doctor couldn't figure out how my skin stretched as far as it did without popping and sending me sputtering into the stratosphere.

Of course, I wouldn't have gained that much weight if I had stayed active, but I plumped my rump deep into the cushions of a chair and sat and ate a good deal of my pregnancy away. In fact, not long after learning of my condition, I developed cravings. I wanted fresh coconut, chocolate pop, and lobster. Truly the grocery list of a pregnant woman. And with the cravings came urgency; so sweet Les would wander into the wee hours searching for ways to fill my odd requests. He found the chocolate soda and the coconut the first night, but the lobster took a number of days and outings to locate. The months of demands I made on Les before our baby's birth should have thrown *him* into labor.

Leslie Martin Clairmont II was born April 15, 1965, to an amazed mommy. Ten days earlier I had turned twenty years old, which disappointed my hopes of being a teenage mom. Don't ask me why that was my goal. I guess I thought it would be "cool."

Marty was born with a full crop of black hair. What a surprise since I was from a family of blonds, but Les's family was French Canadian. Actually, I was expecting a baldheaded girl. So much for my prophetic gift.

The first time Marty was placed in my arms, I was stunned and silenced. I had never seen anything more exquisite. As I stared at his little fingers and ears and touched his dark hair, I thought, *Patsy, this is the first thing you have ever done right.*

Those first moments with my son caused a spiritual awakening within me. As I examined this creation, my fractured heart knew beyond a shadow of a doubt that there was a God. Right then I promised my mother's God that, when I recovered, I would go to church and live differently.

My mothering skills at best were stifling. I was so afraid that the sweetest privilege I'd ever had—of becoming a mom—would be taken from me that I became ridiculously vigilant. I remember after returning home from the hospital I struggled with some after-pregnancy challenges, and a family member offered to take Marty home for a few days. I was angry and hurt to think anyone would want to separate me from my newborn. I thought it a cruel offer.

Marty stopped breathing several times during his infancy, causing several middle-of-the-night crises, as we scurried to emergency rooms. Today, as I think back, I'm not sure Marty was in any danger except from having a mom who overmonitored his every breath.

Les was an ecstatic dad. He loved holding Marty, rocking him, and singing to him day or night. In fact, when Les would come in from work at 11 p.m., he would "accidentally" bump the crib to wake Marty so he could hold him.

Marty grew to be a willful toddler—probably to survive his doting mom. We had battles over *no,* a word he didn't appreciate. One day after telling Marty no, he drew in a deep breath, turned red and violet, and passed out. He was only out for a few moments, but when he awoke he was colorless and limp as a wet washcloth. I rushed him to our doctor, and after a careful examination, Marty was diagnosed with a bad temper.

"Next time Marty holds his breath, usher him over to the sink and flick a little water in his face. That will break the cycle by causing him to catch his breath," the doctor stated with confidence.

Sure enough, it worked. I only had to sprinkle Marty twice, and we had a cure. That is, a cure for his breathholding but not for his stubbornness. Marty was a year old when he toddled over to the oven and put his hand on the hot glass door. I yelled a warning no from across the room, he turned his head toward me to acknowledge my command, and then he put his hand on the glass anyway. It burned Marty's fingertips and made him downright angry; so he put his hand back on the glass again, only to add to his pain. By the time I scampered across the room and grabbed Marty up, his fingertips looked like toasted Rice Krispies because he continued to touch the glass in an attempt to win. I'm not sure to this day that Marty has a clear set of fingerprints on that hand.

Les and I shouldn't have been surprised at Marty's determination because we both were like mules. Of course, I was more aware of Les's stubbornness and vice versa. We both insisted we were right and had to have our own way—although I must admit that Les was more likely to give in. Maybe he should have tried the water flicking treatment on me.

Marty grew up in the worst years of my agoraphobia,

often absorbing my fears and observing my radical behavior. He became a victim of my abnormalities. I can't imagine how he felt as he watched his mom stalk through the house searching for storms out every window and then having to huddle under tables with me because of my fear of tornadoes. His impressionable little heart must have been imprinted with scary confusion.

Therapy should precede the writing of one's autobiography because it sure can stir up a wasps' nest of stinging memories. The most painful is realizing how difficult my behavior must have been for Marty's innocent heart. All I ever wanted to give my son was the best, but all I could give him was who I was at that time. I'm so grateful that Jesus is a Redeemer. And that he is able to do what we can't for our children, regardless of their age. Hope is blessed relief for a mother's broken heart and a child's future welfare.

Marty occasionally made contributions to the frenzy of our home life. At three years old, he ingested a bottle of baby aspirin, which he had maneuvered off a high shelf by standing on a stool and using a golf club. Another day he came into the house screaming, with his face covered in blood. My knees went weak. It turned out he had walked under a tree limb, and a thorn had grazed his head. I had no idea scalps could bleed like that.

Then there was the time he was running across the room with the end of a plastic golf club in his mouth and rammed into the couch. The club handle entered the soft tissue in the back of his mouth and was dangling. By the time I reached Marty, he had yanked out the club, sending forth a gusher of blood. The doctors at first thought he had removed his own tonsils.

And I'm grateful that when Marty accidentally torched his train set while playing with matches he woke me from my nap to tell me. I doused the flames quickly.

Shattering glass alerted me to the time he ran through a glass door. So many glass splinters covered him that I had to vacuum his entire body. Growing up isn't easy—for the child or the parent.

But Marty did grow up; somehow he survived his mishaps and his mom, and he joined the Air Force. He was sent to Guam, where he fell in love with a Korean girl and became engaged. On his return to the States, he made plans for his sweetheart to join him, but she decided moving to America was too overwhelming. Marty was crushed. And for many years, it appeared Marty would remain single.

Actually, I had noted, bachelorhood wasn't in Marty's best interest. He was becoming isolated and insulated. Marty's first name, Leslie, means "gray fortress," and he was becoming one. Then, in a serendipitous moment when Marty was thirty-five, he met a pretty blonde named Patti. I watched a light turn back on in Marty's eyes, witnessed his heart soften, and saw him step out of himself. Marty and Patti married four months later. And while the marriage is only two years old, love clearly makes a difference.

Marty runs a church conference center, where he functions as the camp's architect, builder, handyman, groundskeeper, mechanic, electrician, and administrator. And sometimes he's even the cook. I admire Marty's versatility, loyalty, and honesty. My heart fills with gratitude that out of the ashes of my neurotic, parental attempts, the Lord has brought forth a kind, hardworking, and dedicated man.

Hope is blessed relief for a mother's broken heart and a child's future welfare.

13

Say What?

I'M NOT SURE WHICH CAME FIRST—the backaches, stomachaches, or the cramping—but I was one sick cookie. Then I lost weight and felt nauseous constantly. Repeated doctor's visits and many tests later, we still had no clue as to my ongoing illness. I was becoming thinner, and I couldn't keep any food down; so I lay on the couch, groaning and sucking oranges for a source of moisture. Maybe I was dying.

During one of my many appointments, my doctor stared at the test results that once again showed no answers to my mysterious malady. Finally, he said, "Patsy, I just can't figure out what's wrong."

"Me either," I moaned, as I sat slumped in a nearby chair. "It does seem odd though, that I keep getting skinnier and skinnier while my breasts keep getting bigger and bigger."

The doctor's head jerked up like he had been hit with a

stun gun. Then he jumped up and dashed from the room. A few minutes later the nurse burst into the room and mumbled something about a rabbit. Then she disappeared. A short time later the nurse was back and said simply, "Yep, you are."

"Say what?" I mumbled.

"Pregnant," she said.

"Pregnant?" I was confused. "Pregnant? I'm too old to be pregnant."

"How old are you?" she asked, wide-eyed.

"I'm twenty-eight."

The nurse threw back her head and guffawed.

Les, upon receiving the news, looked like a Cheshire cat . . . for months. He couldn't stop smiling. I was nervously, nauseously, overjoyed.

I already was having a problem with spotting, which concerned the doctor, who immediately limited my activities. He told me I couldn't do steps. We lived in a second-floor apartment at a Youth for Christ camp; so I could see we had a challenge. I imagined being hoisted up and down on pulleys for the next six months. Good luck to the hoisters!

As the baby grew within me, he pressed on my sciatic nerve. This added to the dynamics of our home life because you could hear me scream like a banshee when that nerve sent lightning strikes through my leg. The good news was by the time the shriek was out of my mouth, the pain was gone. It kept my family startled, like living with a short-circuited smoke detector.

126

Say What?

Unlike my pregnancy with Marty, I didn't crave odd foods. I wasn't that select. Once my nausea passed, I ate everything that wasn't secured until my hips felt more like well-stocked saddlebags. I was grateful that, while I was speaking fairly regularly in my local area, I wasn't taking long trips. Somehow, my speaking and pregnancy managed to coexist, which is more than I could say for the pregnancy and me!

Along my pregnancy path I waddled into Lamaze classes. Well, all but the last two sessions. Here's my advice: Don't miss the last two.

My first contraction was a surprise. Oh, I knew it was time because my water had broken an hour earlier, but instead of regular labor pains, I had back labor. As soon as the first contraction circled around my body and concluded in my spine, I was up searching for the labor handbook. Sure enough, they had a chapter on back labor. I sat down with Les, and we went over what he could do to help when the pains became more intense.

The book suggested we take a deck of cards along to pass time between contractions. The author obviously didn't attend the same church as my mom. Cards can be a good diversion during labor, but only with salt and pepper. I found the diamonds weren't bad, but the spades and clubs were bland. When labor turned lively, I was twisting and biting down on anything within reach. The three of hearts was definitely a tad tart.

When Jason Robert Clairmont was born, nine years after

Marty, we were grateful and blessed. Jason entered the world with a suntan. Later I learned it was jaundice, but he wore it well. Unlike his brother's head of thick black hair, Jason was sporting a light shock of red hair. He was a passive baby—until we arrived home. Then Jason decided to test his limits, as he howled through three months of colic. I thought of exchanging him for a collie, but I had allergies.

Overnight the colic left, and the sweetest baby a parent would ever want appeared. Jason took two separate two-hour naps a day, slept through the night, and kept a perpetual smile on his face. People asked if it was painted on.

For several years after he was born, I didn't know Jason's name meant "peacemaker," but it couldn't have been more accurate, unless you asked Marty. Marty, a dyed-in-the-wool only child, was married to his exclusivity and his privacy. Peacemaker or not, to Marty, Jason reeked of intrusion. I tried creative strategies like incorporating Marty as Mommy's helper and then celebrating his involvement and his new brotherhood.

But Marty read me like a dog-eared book. One day he announced, "If you think all those nice things you're saying are going to make me like that baby better, you're wrong." Oops. The family unity stretched out before us like the Sahara.

Eventually Marty became an involved and protective brother, but I still wasn't certain he wouldn't trade Jason for a bag of marbles or a flea collar. Since then I've learned such tension is common between siblings. My brother would have jubilantly given me to the gypsies; he just didn't know any. Somehow those raucous feelings eventually mellow, as we wade through the strong bonds of daily living side by side. The true cure comes when a sibling leaves home and lives out in the world a while; life experiences often cause us to cherish family more.

Spurred by my regret of having had such a melancholy approach with Marty as a young child, I made a promise during my second pregnancy that regardless how I felt I would greet my baby each morning with joy. That discipline benefited our entire family.

Jason was a well-behaved child. A single word or look was usually all he needed to set him on a proper course. Even from a young age, eating and resting were two of his favorite pastimes.

Jason was as much a daddy's boy as he was a momma's boy. He seemed to come equipped with bipartisan flair. Jason was adaptable and adorable . . .

. . . unless you set lima beans or salmon patties in front of him. Then adorable drained out quickly. Jason transformed into stone boy. He would sit stoically for hours without ingesting even a nibble of a bean or an itsy-bitsy bite of salmon. No doubt remained that the kid could sit a good chair.

In elementary school, Jason played baseball. Well, "played" might be an exaggeration. He preferred to watch the ball as it whizzed passed him again and again. He had figured out that, if he didn't swing at all, he had a good chance of making it to first base. Definitely not a risktaker, Jason waited it out, which is why one season he was given the award for being on base more than any other player. Actually, by high school he was a good, all-around athlete, and yes, he swung his bat and maintained a high average.

Jason's peacemaking personality was obvious. I remember when he had the chicken pox (for the second time), the teacher said the whole class missed him so much that it became a distraction, and she finally had everyone write Jason get-well letters to help settle them down. Another elementary teacher told me whenever she had a hot spot in her classroom, with kids bickering, she would move Jason into the middle of it, and soon the dissension dissipated. Les and I were fascinated with our little peacemaker since, when we were in school, we would have been the ones causing the squabble.

We realized Jason definitely was our son when we attended a parent-teacher meeting. The teacher announced Jason was flunking her course. I was irritated that she had waited so long to alert us to the problem. She then produced a letter she had sent home weeks earlier that had been signed by my husband. Except it wasn't Les's signature, it was Jason's imitation of Les's signature. Our little peacemaker was now our little forger. To increase the hope that Jason wouldn't take up the wrong future occupation, his dad had a, ahem, motivational moment with him. I'm grateful to say that Jason emerged believing that peacemaking was a far more honorable route.

Jason met his future wife, Danya, when they were sixteen. She was a stunning brunette with a bouncy personality. Once they spotted each other, they never considered anyone else. They dated for five years and then chose to wed in the autumn of 1995.

The night before the wedding, trouble started to brew. At the rehearsal dinner Jason became ill; I had never seen him so sick. He left the dinner early and went home to bed.

Then the winds picked up, and the temperature dropped. In the morning, we learned the winds had blown down the tent we had rented to extend the church's reception area. And if that wasn't enough, because of the cold snap, we needed to rig up a heater for the tent.

That day the tent people made their repairs in the nick of time and brought a heater that made it toasty for our guests. But when I arrived for the service, the wedding prompter had disappeared. You know, she's the one who tells everyone where to be and when to walk down the aisle. She probably was carried off by the wind. I nabbed a friend who graciously took on the role.

Jason's health had improved, but he still was pale and weak. I was in the front row during the service watching him as he wobbled gently to and fro. But my attention was drawn away when I noticed one of his groomsmen was covered in beads of sweat and looked suspiciously green. Then I realized Marty was leaning forward in the pew, as if he were going to leap into the wedding party. That was when I spotted Danya's brother, another groomsman, had locked his knees and was teetering back and forth as though he was going to pass out. Marty was waiting to see in which direction Derrick was going to faint so he could catch him.

"Lord, help!" my heart cried, as my eyes flitted from person to person, wondering who was going to topple first. Much to my amazement, the guys made it through the wedding. Ceremonies are definitely hard on men.

As Jason and Danya drove off for their honeymoon, I sighed with relief. Even though there were potential glitzes galore we not only survived, it was one of the happiest days of my life.

Today I love watching Jason and Danya interact. Even after eight years of marriage, they remain playful and thoughtful, and take each other's interests to heart.

When two are joined together, often more is the loving result. And our blessed more is Justin and Noah, our grandsons. Justin is three years old at the time of this writing, and Noah is six months. They have added both joy and vigor to our existence.

Justin is so unlike his daddy in temperament. This little live wire is a bundle of sassy intentions. It's fun for me to observe the two together. Justin occasionally tries to flip his daddy's switch to rile him, but calm Jason smiles and out-waits Justin's feisty schemes.

Noah is an armload of smiles. He has a sunny disposition—as long as he's full. Keep him tanked up, and he's all giggles and joy. It's a blast from the past for me because Jason and Noah look like Tic and Tac. When Jason holds Noah, we all giggle over how someone so big and someone so small could look so alike.

When folks say grandparenting is the best, they are underestimating the experience. It's over-the-top to glimpse your future in the lives of your children's children. Hope is multigenerational.

I've enjoyed watching my son's journey into manhood and fatherhood. Jason is a faithful husband, a nurturing father, and a gentle son. I'm not surprised because he's inclined to stay close to his family, and Les set a strong example of a father's loving involvement. I appreciate and admire my peacemaking son's tender-hearted and protective ways.

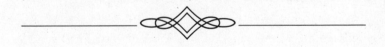

Hope is multigenerational.

14

Real Estate

*I*F I HAD BECOME A REAL-ESTATE BROKER, oh, say, when I was five years old, I would be a baroness today. Between my moving-on mother and my let's-go husband, I've lived in enough different homes to qualify me for gypsy-ship. And we've needed a ship at times to move our belongings. Make that a cargo ship 'cause, honey, we've got stuff.

Of course, folks naturally figure, if you move all the time, muddled messes are eliminated, but I would be an exception to that belief. Even with multiple moves, we U-Haul our clutter from location to location.

When I was growing up, my parents never moved state-to-state, just school-district-to-school-district. So by the time I made it to ninth grade, I had attended nine schools and lived in seven houses. I guess Mom unknowingly was preparing me for my nomad husband. Les and I have been married for forty-one years, and at last count we have moved thirty-plus times.

A few of those moves were transitional moves before the official moves but nonetheless required packing and repacking.

Speaking of packing, one would think I would be a pro by now. Not so. Proof of that pudding would be when I recently found a missing piece of jewelry tucked in the Christmas ornaments. I have learned not to file any lost claims until I've lived in a place long enough to unpack all the boxes, which, to date, has never happened.

One of the challenges of a mobile life is that, along our path, we have misplaced a slew of items. Big items, things that you would wonder how a person could go off and leave—like my wedding dress, an ornately framed print, an aquarium with pumps, and even, get this, a riding lawn mower. Now that's not easy.

But then neither is frequent moving. Golly, I wish I could earn frequent house miles, which by now should qualify me to fly free to, say, Pluto and back. Of course that would mean I'd have to pack again. Besides, with my luck, while we were there, Les would find a nice plot of land overlooking Mars and want to buy it for a vacation home. I considered having dollies affixed to the undersides of all our furniture just to expedite our next move regardless of which planet we chose.

Despite all the moving, Les and I have only lived outside of Michigan once, and that was when we first married. We rented a basement apartment in an old Kentucky mansion that looked like it was straight out of an episode of *The Addams Family.* That hideous experience included roaches, rats, and a landlady who looked strangely like Uncle Festus. But we had spent our last dollars to rent the place, so we had to stick it out. Les spent every other night at the barracks, which meant those nights I was left alone in that infested dungeon. That was one of the few times in our married life that I was grateful to move. A true reality check for a seventeen-year-old bride who thought she would live happily ever after in a castle turret, not the dungeon.

Several of our homes were on campgrounds because Les was employed as a maintenance man and a camp director. Those were wonderful experiences because they offered our family exposure to people from all walks of life and the benefits of lakes, land, and horses. We lived at three different camp facilities in four different houses, and one of the houses we lived in twice.

Recycling a previous house is strange. It's like, after years, trying on your wedding gown to find it just doesn't seem to fit the way it once did.

We didn't stay long the second time though. A house across the lake became available after just a few months, and once again we packed up and moved. I'm surprised our belongings didn't have skid marks on them from packing and unpacking them so frequently.

The "new" house was small, but in need of big help, which we weren't in a position to offer it. So it was an "as is" deal. But while the inside had a rumpled look, the views outside were wonderful, and we delighted in them. We had a five-acre lake out our front window and a wildlife sanctuary next to us. Some folks, who obviously lacked vision, thought it was a swamp.

What I loved about that house, beside the views, was the flood of natural light that poured in through the multiple windows. What I disliked was the tissue-thin carpet, the one tiny bathroom, and the thousands of carpenter ants that moved in and used our ductwork as their superhighway. If only I could have set up a tollbooth.

Once we discovered the ants were congregating in the core of our bedroom door, we waited until evening, when they had gathered from the four corners of our ducts, then we unhinged the door and dragged it away . . . far away, into a different zip code. Then, evidently inspired by giving the ants a new location, we moved too.

It would be difficult for me to say which has been my favorite place to live because each one offered something different. One house featured a big, stone fireplace, another had a walk-in kitchen pantry, one was a secluded country hideaway, another was a city apartment, one had multiple gardens, and then there was the one with a floor plan that looked like a bowling alley.

I did so love our North Second Street home, the only one I pushed to get. Of course, being married to ready-to-relocate Les, I didn't have to push hard; it was more like a slight nudge. As soon as I entered the front door, I knew it was my dream. The house was cottagelike with lots of garden space in the backyard. The cove ceilings, wide baseboards, leaded glass windows, and hardwood floors fit comfortably with who I was. Plus the rooms were petite and lent themselves to cozy living. Our furniture fit like it was meant to be. We were a perfect match, and I believed it was our until-glory home. Then, after three years, you got it, we moved.

Growing up, my favorite house was on Mansfield Street. My fondness for it had nothing to do with the house, even though it was lovely, but rather the memory of receiving my first bicycle while we lived there.

I thought it unkind, on the morning of my eighth birthday, that my parents made me go outside to retrieve the newspaper. I figured it was my day to be pampered; so I obeyed while I grumbled. I had no idea my dad had set a new bike on the porch. When I stepped through the door, I saw my spiffy gift. I still remember my surprise followed by shouts of jubilation.

A house, room, or neighborhood can bring back a rush of feelings and thoughts we hadn't considered in years. In fact, if you're like me, you're surprised by how much you remember and how fresh your emotions from long ago still are.

One day I was walking through an antique store, when I stopped in my tracks. There was a doll wardrobe exactly like I had when I was a child. We lived at the Mansfield house when I received it as a Christmas gift from Santa. I was seven. I hadn't thought about that case since I was a kid, but a flood of remembrance ran down the store's aisle and rushed over me. The wardrobe opened up like a trunk, and inside was a place to hang clothes, store your doll, and put smaller items in a drawer. On the front a Scottie dog was emblazoned. I was going to buy it just because it made me feel so good, but the owner was asking too much. Oh, well, I loved the rush of déjà vu it afforded me.

An item that I remember without stimulus was our picnic basket. I don't know when Mom bought it, but I clearly remember the wire basket with the black handles that she used for our trips to the park. Mom always lined it with newspapers to insulate it so the prepared hot foods would stay warm and so we didn't leave a trail of silverware on our walk to the picnic tables. Dad would pack up the forest green Coleman tabletop cookstove and off we would go. Oh, yes, and the green, collapsible cup. That was the most fun because I'd play with it all the way to our destination. By the time we pulled into the park, the cup was catawampus from my working it in and out like an accordion. Even though Mom loved to change houses and hairdos, she was married to that picnic basket. It stayed in our family for years—at least five houses—toted faithfully from one abode to another. And even though as a child I didn't particularly care for picnics, I sure liked that basket. Maybe because it, like I, survived the transitory system.

For many people, moving around is a grand experience, but when you're fragile and insecure, it can add to your dilemma. By the time we lived in one spot for a while, my undeveloped root system would try to splay and take hold, which seemed to be a sure sign we were going to move soon.

One of the aspects of life I've struggled with most is feeling that I belonged. Whether it was my emotionally distant dad or my Northernness despite having a Southern heritage, my tagalong relationship with my brother, or my mother's emotional departure during the times she was down, belonging was an issue that I had a hard time settling in my heart. As a youngster, even though I was outspoken, I found it difficult to begin anew with teachers and friends. Of course, it didn't help that I was and am directionally deficient, which made learning new neighborhoods and school floor plans tricky. I notice I still get edgy when left on my own in a new setting.

During my agoraphobic years, our constant moves were jarring emotionally for me. Change felt threatening, and the disruption of gathering up our belongings was disconcerting. Not to mention trying to reposition everything again in a functional manner when I wasn't even functional myself.

I always wanted to stay put, yet as I look back over all our house-cavorting years, I must say it has made for a textured life map. One thing moving frequently can do for you is help you not to hold on too tight, and the Lord knew I needed to loosen my white-knuckled grip. Besides, if I hadn't moved around so much, I doubt if I'd have been prepared for the highly mobile lifestyle I live today. I travel more than thirty weekends a year and stay mainly in hotels, most of which I'd like to clean and decorate before I turn in. Hotel-hopping has convinced me there truly is no place like home.

I've met folks who have lived in only two or three houses

their entire lives. I think that sounds heavenly. It sounds anchoring. It sounds abnormal. That's the thing about repetition—you do something long enough, and it becomes norm.

A house is more than a place to put up our feet and watch television. It represents belonging in that it offers us placement on this crowded globe. Have you ever met anyone who didn't sooner or later ask, "Where do you live?" A home represents our most significant relationships. It offers us refuge from the storms and the banditos. It's where we dine in each other's presence. It's the place that shelters our privacy and guards our family members. It holds our stuff, it's where our friends come to share, and it's where, at the end of a day, we can lock the door and sleep in peace. A home helps to identify us to an inquisitive world. From the street name to the house numbers a home shouts, "She belongs here!" So I guess I've experienced more "belonging" than most folks have. Hope, for me, is realizing one day I'll have a mansion in glory, and I'll never have to move again.

Meanwhile . . .

Hope, for me, is realizing one day I'll have a mansion in glory, and I'll never have to move again!

15
String of Pearls

AFTER MY MOTHER-IN-LAW DIED, I was given a string of her pearls. I loved wearing them, because I felt they kept Lena close. One day, as I was leaving my hotel room to check out, my strand of precious pearls broke. Pearls flew everywhere—down the hall, behind plants, and into doorways. I was beside myself, because I was already running late for my flight, and yet I didn't want to leave without Lena's pearls. I scooped up as many as I could find and hurried to the airport. On the way I comforted myself with the thought that the lost pearls could be replaced and the found ones restrung.

When I think back on those pearls flying wildly in all directions, I can't help but think of my erratic emotions that flew around for years leaving me all unstrung. I'm grateful the Lord came to my rescue and helped me collect them so he could restring me. Along with the newly strung emotions, he added some other beautiful pearls to the string: friends.

Friends help us to journey through life on the right path, which is what makes them so valuable, like precious pearls. Some friends have walked beside me, some have warned me of dangerous drop-offs ahead, and some have offered a hand-up when the next step was too high for Little Me. But one thing puzzles me about some of my friends: They hate to shop, even for pearls. (I wonder if surgery could correct that?) Trust me, I wouldn't fit in that catalog. My shopper-parts are well oiled and finely tuned. I can be almost comatose with exhaustion—that is, until you position me at the front door of a mall. Then watch out! I become wildly aerobic.

When I look back on the path I've trod, I realize I've come a long way, baby, from the days I was afraid to go shopping until now when Les is afraid I will go . . . again. Now I have to guard my liberty that I don't use it as a license to be excessive.

That brings me to the day I met The Mall of America in Bloomington, Minnesota. It draws visitors from all over the world. Imagine, five hundred stores under one massive roof and me a former agoraphobic. When Women of Faith did a conference near the megamall, I couldn't resist dropping in for a look-see.

Well, it happened that Leigh Cappillino, our worship leader, was leaving our hotel for the mall the same time as I. We decided to take a cab together so we could share the expense, with the agreement that we would go our own ways when we arrived. Later we discovered that neither of us thought the other could keep up.

The cab driver dropped us off at Nordstrom's because we both wanted to start our shopping tour there. As the cabbie sped away, Leigh and I both headed for the shoe department. After a thorough investigation of that department, we made a beeline for the clothing department, where we kept meeting on every other aisle. Then we both confessed a need to go to the third floor for lingerie, which turned into a giggle fest. Soon we agreed we were famished and needed some sustenance, which is when we realized we were a mean, lean shopping machine team. After our salads, we returned to the clothing department and made a final visit to the shoes.

Leigh and I found we were compatible in our shopping styles: eat rapidly, restroom rarely, and shop, shop, shop. She and I made friends of the sales staff as we cavorted from floor to floor. Actually, I think they found us labor intensive, but they sweetly indulged us.

At one point in our trek I was trying on a turtleneck, slacks, and a bomber jacket, while Leigh was across the hall trying on half the tops and jeans on the second floor. I could hear Leigh in a gab session, but I couldn't figure out who the recipient of her Southern flair was.

I stepped into the hall just as a young saleswoman, Lisa, rounded the corner with another armload of clothes for

Leigh to try on. Lisa looked at the changing room from which the rousing chatter was bubbling forth and glanced at me with a question in her eyes: *Who is she talking to?*

I shrugged my shoulders, giggling. Lisa and I stood together, fascinated that anyone could have that much to talk about all by herself. No wonder Leigh can shop alone. Personally, I enjoy a friend's opinion when I'm stuck, oh, say, between the polka-dotted hiphuggers or the fringed, leather bell-bottoms.

Leigh is one of the most sanguine shoppers I've ever met, especially the way she chats with herself the whole time she's flipping through the racks. Okay, okay, I sometimes talk to myself, too, but I'm old. Leigh isn't halfway through her thirties.

(Now that I think about it, that's brilliant, because when Leigh gets to be my age and talks to herself, her friends will say, "Oh, she's always done that." Hmmm, that's smart, Leigh.)

By the end of the spree, I decided one had not truly shopped until she went with Leigh. She knows how to boogie through an aisle.

Oh, did I mention we never left Nordstrom's? Uh huh. More than five hundred stores, and we stayed where we had begun . . . for nine and a half hours. Yep, nine and a half. I told you we were shoppers. (I wonder if surgery could correct that?)

We left the store slaphappy and satisfied. The time flew for Leigh and me, which is what happens when you're with a friend.

But friends aren't just sisters who journey to the mall with us. Sisters-in-the-Lord also laugh with us along the way, making the trek easier by their very presence. Several years ago, my editor, Janet, and I needed to pull away from life's pressures to concentrate on a book I was writing. So a friend of mine offered her compound in northern Michigan as a getaway for Janet and me. When we arrived, we found the house had everything to make life cozy—a fireplace, a big dining room table, and comfy chairs that looked out over the woods where the deer pranced through, the wild turkeys noisily paraded, and two swans glided on a nearby lake.

But one item in the house was disconcerting: a real bearskin rug. We knew it was real because the head was still attached. We found the bear's eyes, his big nose, and his snarly teeth unsettling. So we turned our backs to him and set up workstations on the dining room table.

A short time later, I walked across the room to the Kleenex box and somehow tripped over the bear (he probably reached up and grabbed me). Once I had recovered my balance, Janet and I were aghast to discover the bear's tongue had flown across the room and was lying, way too lifelike, on the floor. Ew! Worse yet, we immediately realized we needed to get it back into his mouth. Double ew! Picking it up with a Kleenex, I darted across the room and sort of flung it into his mouth. As his tongue lolled to one side, we burst out laughing. The bear looked as if he had a hangover. So I arranged the, uh, item several different ways, none of which looked natural—out in front, more to the back, maybe a little to the side. Why hadn't we studied this part of his anatomy a little closer? Of course, by this time we were in fits of laughter.

If I had been by myself, this wouldn't have been nearly as much fun. Actually, it wouldn't have been fun at all. But having a gem of a friend with you can make all the difference.

Our sisters help us in other ways, too. Jan Frank and Ginny Lukei have added the pearls of safety of truth and accountability to my life. We met fifteen years ago, and our friendships have endured physical distance and extended absences. (They live in California, and I live in Michigan). We have helped each other through fiery trials and unexpected losses.

Ginny has been in a circumstantial valley for several years now. It's a pit, actually. Yet I've watched her respond by lacing up her sandals and choosing to take calculated steps in the direction of righteousness. Severe family health issues, a major house fire, unexpected financial pressures, selling her home, two temporary physical moves, and living in the havoc of remodeling have all been her recent lot in life. It's a lot she would gladly sell . . . cheap. Occasionally the strain of Ginny's ongoing struggles weighs her down, but she is fast to call for counsel and prayer support because she understands the Lord has given us each other for those high purposes.

Understanding that maturity is a path in this life, like the seemingly endless Appalachian Trail, rather than a particular location, like Topeka, Kansas, gives me hope to press on even after I fail, fall, and have forgotten the way. And it enables me to encourage others, like Ginny, to do the same.

Sometimes, though, friendships lose their pearly luster and add to our bulging sack of sorrows—sorrows we all collect if we live on this terra firma for more than a month. Think how many people were once your friends but are no longer in your life. Sure, some moved, died, or took on a demanding new path, but others represent rejection, misunderstanding, betrayal, and offense. It's hard to even think of them without a sense of hurt, loss, bitterness, loneliness, and regret. I know. Sometimes, in friendship, pressures can cause the strand to break.

Many years ago I ended a relationship with someone who had been a strong example of a godly woman in my life. I learned much under her tutelage. But after several years, we had some misunderstandings that bred hurt and mistrust between us. It was easier for me to walk away than to do the work of talking out our differences. I now regret my choice. She has since moved away, and I've lost contact with her, making it impossible to revisit the choices I initially made. I wish I'd had the maturity to take responsibility for my part in our conflict and to extend grace to her for what I saw as her part. We still may have chosen to part company, but it would have been on a much more honorable plane.

I'm grateful that, even when I've been the offender, God has redeemed my mistakes and made them my hall monitors so that I can grow wiser and more loving and value people over pride. I realize that, here on earth, not everyone was meant to stay in our lives for extended lengths of time. I have to remind myself of that because basically I want everyone I care for to always be a part of my string of pearls. Some folks just breeze through; others settle in for a season and then move on; a few hunker down for the long haul. Those who settle in for a lifetime do so not necessarily because they are braver, more loving, or even more loyal, but because they were meant to. It was part of the plan. So those who have left us must also be considered part of the ultimate plan.

Sometimes a friend can change so much that we don't fit together as well as we once did. Even the most positive of adjustments can be a threat if it changes the dynamics of a relationship. Also, one person may outgrow the other. It's not that they become better than the other, but their compatibility is altered to the degree that both become uncomfortable. And some relationships become unhealthy to the point that we need to back away for a season or more.

Certainly, the pain a relationship causes us can force us to see ourselves in a new and sometimes unflattering but honest light. From her book, *The Heart of Prayer for Women of Faith,* Lana Bateman, our Women of Faith chaplain, shares, "At one of our Women of Faith Conferences, a middle-aged mother described the pain she had suffered through the alcoholism of her youngest daughter. After sharing with her about 'seeking God's heart,' she agreed to ask how the Lord might have her pray for this adult child.

"The next day I had occasion to see her for a brief moment. She shared what had happened when she took her request to God the night before. Surprisingly, he did not ask her to pray for the daughter's release from alcohol or for the counseling she so obviously needed. Instead, as she meditated on the situation, he impressed her to confess her own struggles with addictive behavior. This dismantled any condemning thoughts she held toward her daughter. Then he led her to pray that her youngest child would have an encounter with him, that the walls of denial would be destroyed, and that he might speak truth into her life."

When we trigger each other's hostility, encourage each other's weakness, or spend most of our time trying to patch up hurt feelings, we need a break. Often some distance can bring greater objectivity, allowing us to reenter each other's space at a better place.

One of my many house moves was exciting, but it ended up shaking me to the core. I felt misplaced and panicky. I couldn't find my emotional bearings. Instead of recognizing my fears, I became angry and shot barbs in all directions. A friend, who grew tired of debarbing herself, stepped away from our friendship until I worked through my anger. Initially I was offended and felt betrayed by what seemed like her lack of support. But after a while I came to grips with my insecurities, my expectations, and my disappointments. Then I was grateful she had backed away, because that gave me the space I needed to work through my own tangled emotions, and it forced me to stop blaming others for my own stuff. It wasn't her job to fix me, and it wasn't my place to judge her.

I wasn't initially aware that the move had hit me at my most vulnerable spot: belonging. I didn't purpose to be unkind, but nonetheless I was. I wanted others to rescue me, and when they didn't, I felt misled, misunderstood, and rejected. Jesus is our rescuer, and when we depend on others, we set ourselves up for misunderstandings and hurt. I know I did.

I chose to write about relationships as part of my life's story because friendships have been extremely important to me. They offer me a reflection of myself that I might otherwise miss. Yet I haven't found them easy. The Scriptures speak of doing "the hard work of getting along with each other" (James 3:18), and for me it has been laborious. People expose our inconsistencies, which can feel threatening. And folks can wear on our nerves, especially if our nerves are too close to the surface. At any point folks also can choose to betray us or walk out on us, which leaves us emotionally defenseless. One of the lessons I desperately needed to learn was that I couldn't expect my sisters, regardless of how divine they were, to meet my deep needs.

Because of the priceless investment friends have made in my life, I chose Milk 'n' Honey for my ministry's name. It spoke to me of companionship and exuded promise. I saw the milk as being nurturing, like a well-nourished child whose body and bones have grown strong or as a child of God who is suckled by the Scriptures. The honey for me represented sweet encouragement—something we all need.

In the book of Exodus, the Israelites were directed toward

the Promised Land, a land described as flowing with *milk and honey*. Isn't that an enriching picture of prosperity, one that flows with provision? By its very properties it proclaims, *Better days are coming*. That's what I want to broadcast to women: *Hope is just ahead!* I know the effort I had to expend to make it across the desert of depression. It was like trying to cross the Sahara in rubber boots. Change isn't without cost, and maturity is deepened by hardship.

I never expected to have a ministry to others. I didn't have a personal agenda to become a speaker or an author. Why, I had trouble believing I could make it to a Kroger's to buy groceries for my family. Doing what I do today is way beyond me, but then God's plans always flourish more beautifully than ours. Of course, his work within us is to enlarge our hearts with his expansive presence. How he accomplishes that in each of us is as varied as the shapes of clouds in the heavens.

I don't believe for a moment that I was sent out onto the highways and byways of life because I was healed and whole and ready to go. I was tattered, willful, and wounded. Yet I believe the Lord sent me out that I might learn what it means to seek healing and walk toward wholeness. And God knew I needed to be accountable and nurtured by believers. Besides, if the Lord had waited until I integrated his restorative truths before he released me to minister, I'd probably be sitting in Egypt inside a pyramid trying to decipher the hieroglyphics of my life. Instead, he sent me out in my inadequacy to learn of his sufficiency. In my obvious weaknesses, I stumbled toward God that I might walk in the protection of his holy stride. And in my knee-knocking resistance, he nudged me forward that I might find his steady liberty.

At times the Lord has chosen to use a friend to steady me when I've teetered, and while I've been grateful, I also know not to expect that to always be the case. The next time, God might allow me to fall, to suffer the consequences of my actions, because my perspective from that lowly place could expand my capacity to be more gracious to others. Besides, a set of skinned knees can be a lasting reminder to maintain a good focus. For me, failure has been a strict teacher of God's mercies, a curriculum I wouldn't volunteer for, yet a class I can't afford to miss.

From what the class has taught me so far, I've learned that a milk and honey existence is a life lived out in hope, based on a defined sense of self in Christ and on a willingness to unselfishly and wisely invest in others' lives.

Hope's road is endless. And, thank heaven, it has pearls along the way.

Hope's road is endless.

16
Scripted Hope

MY FIFTY-NINE YEARS OF LIFE have consisted of deep valleys and high mountain peaks, and at this juncture, I wouldn't want to give up the view I've gained from both. Sometimes we don't see the Lord's hand guiding us until after the fact, as we note that all the dots connected and the finished piece is picture perfect. That's certainly the case for me.

Not that I've arrived. I still have tedious moments, bouts of insecurity, and sad days, but they don't paralyze me like they once did. Nor do they send me plunging into panic and despair. Sometimes I have a fresh battle with an old fear, but nowadays the clash is short-lived, and the result is victory.

Recently Les took an extended trip, leaving me home alone, which was fine; I'm a big girl now. That is, until it got dark, which is when Big Me shrunk down smaller than a nervous gnat. Actually, I was doing fine at being brave until in the middle of the first night alone I awoke to our security alarm screaming. Not certain what to do, I tripped out of my room and wobbled through the hall to the kitchen where the security base was located. I figured that, if I met hoodlums on the way, one look at my bedhead and they would flee. Finally, after pounding on every button on the keypad, I figured out how to turn off the alarm (or I killed the thing). That's when I noticed the system's screen was flashing a message that the battery was dead. Relieved, I went back to bed. And while the alarm was fairly easy to shut off, my mind wasn't. I kept thinking of "what ifs." What if someone really was in the house? What if a burglar sneaked in now that the alarm wasn't working? What if . . . After my heart was jumping from the stimulus of my own imaginations, I gave myself a firm lecture, reminded myself of God's superintending of my life, and fell back asleep.

An hour later I awoke to a series of short screeching sounds. Mind you, in the three years we've lived in this house, neither of these things had ever happened. I once again rose up and went in search of the sound. Eventually, as I stumbled around in the dark, I found the culprit—a smoke detector that needed a new battery. Its high-pitched chirping sounded like a herd of soprano crickets. I couldn't figure out how to change the battery so I closed all the doors between it and my bed, stuck my head under a pillow, and tried to fall back asleep, which I eventually did. Now, honey, that's victory.

Had those night noises occurred years ago, the scenario

would have been very different. First, I wouldn't have even tried to stay home alone. But if no family members could be with me, I'd have employed armed chaperons. That, though, would have helped little. If a siren had wailed, I would have outscreeched it by many decibels. Not to mention all the additional folks I would have alerted to rescue me—CSI and a SWAT team. I was a high-drama, high-maintenance queen. Now I'm a peaceful, passive princess.

Okay, maybe not, but I'm far more sane in my responses, and today my first cry is to the Lord. I've learned he's the only one who can recharge my batteries so I can function the way he intended.

Yes, I grew up little, but gratefully I found hope in a big God. One who understands my frailty and isn't offended by my littleness. His expansive plans include my sanity, stability, and personal dignity. It brings the Lord God joy when we long to know him in the smallest parts of our lives that he might grow us up.

I didn't realize the Lord would use my failures to teach me compassion for other strugglers, my fears to teach me about courage that goes beyond feelings, or my foibles to teach me of my limitations and his limitlessness. I viewed my agoraphobic years as wasted and forever lost, but God never wastes anything. Instead, he chooses to rebuild ruins.

Many times women come up to me at conferences to confess their greatest weaknesses or fears, and many times I have understood their dilemma because I too had walked that dark path. To say to another, "I know how you feel," when you've never been where they are, is insulting; but to say, "I've been there," when you really have, and you know the way out, is to run up a banner of hope over their "ruins."

When I attended Recovery meetings over thirty years ago and heard the fragile participants reveal the nitty-gritty struggles of their hearts, I felt as if my air-hungry lungs had received oxygen. I left that meeting feeling as though I had a future. The participants gave me the wondrous gift of encouragement through their honesty and humility. The banner of hope had been raised.

I remember one man, Forrest, sharing in a meeting that he had allowed a simple oversight by another person to churn up such a seething anger within him that he had to be rushed to the hospital because he thought he was having a heart attack. Forrest made several trips to the hospital for heart attacks he never had. But he eventually learned how to deal with his anger before it became fury.

A woman named Gayle told of overmonitoring her health until she became a flaming hypochondriac. Through Recovery she learned to take care of herself but not indulge in neurotic overkill.

Others told of facing their fears (riding in cars, being in storms, riding elevators, etc.), and with each admission my courage grew to face my own fractured behavior. Their vulnerability and their progress brought hope to my skittish heart.

I so wanted God to make my recovery from being an agoraphobic speedy. What purpose could be served by dragging out such a restricting and debilitating disorder? Wasn't it a waste of good time? Of God's time? "Hurry" was my constant plea. But I experienced no instant cures, no overnight remedies, and no immediate miracles. Yet my recovery has been miraculous. Where I was mistaken was in limiting miracles to instantaneous ones. Some of us are slowly unfolding miracles; yet miracles nonetheless. In God's timing and for his purposes, he has accomplished his work in me. And I'm grateful he continues the work. He knew I'd falter and question.

Someone once said, "Courage is fear that has said its prayers." That resonates within me. I do many things today not because I feel brave, but because I have prayed and God has answered and met me with his strength in my utter weakness.

I don't know what sends shudders down your spine, what threatens your security, what gnaws at your worth, but my prayer is that my story will bring you hope, even if it's just the size of a breadcrumb—enough for you to take the next liberating step. I've learned that life is exceedingly difficult and that God is amazingly big. He will reign over our greatest losses, rectify our worst failures, and remedy our deepest insecurities.

I don't understand all the ways of the Lord, but then I'm not suppose to. Faith carries us through life's unknowns and God's mysteries. But one day, one absolutely glorious day I will "get it," and more importantly I'll see Jesus face to face.

That irrepressible hope keeps me breathing deeply, walking faithfully, and singing triumphantly. Little Me has found her big God more than ample to sustain even the wobbliest amongst us.

Yes, I grew up little, but gratefully
I found hope in a big God.

A Conversation with
Patsy Clairmont

by Mary Graham

Mary Graham, president of *Women of Faith,* recently spent a
evening with Patsy to talk about her new book and what it was like
to write a memoir that documented her life and spiritual journey.
Let's listen in . . .

MG: What was it like to write your life story?
PC: It sure stirred up a lot of emotions, I'll tell you that. I found it exhil-
arating and exhausting. It was at times a blessing and at times a very
painful experience. I hadn't realized a lot of things about relationships
with family members—things that I thought were more developed—
until I put the pen to the paper and realized it wasn't quite what I'd
thought. That amazed me. I hadn't recognized that I'd never tried before
to put it into words—what that person felt about me or how deep the
relationship had been. I guess, when you consider they're family, you
think it all connects, and then you begin to realize that sometimes there
is not as much connection as you'd thought. That was surprising to me.
And yet I was also blessed by the fact that there were so many sweet
things with each member of my family that are still so dear to me. It's
fresh all over again. I realized *Oh I miss that person* or *I love that person.*

MG: If you had it to do over again, would you write the book?
PC: My first thought is *Heavens no,* and then my second thought is
Heavens yes! I think it was a divine appointment for me, something
that God intended for me to do. I also think the push that God
used was you, Mary, when you trailed me on this for a long, long
time before I finally heard you with receptive ears. I think subcon-
sciously I knew it would be difficult.

MG: Would you recommend it to others, writing their story that is?
PC: Yes, but I'd say have a therapist nearby! I'd say go for it, but know it will climb right into your mind and emotions and kind of tiptoe around in your heart. I think that even if you weren't going to have it published it would be a good therapy tool.

MG: You were very honest about your struggles and the places you felt you had failed. That had to be painful to go through some of those experiences again. What do you hope people will learn from your story?
PC: I think they will learn about *God's* irrepressible *hope*. My hope is that they'll realize that God is able when we are not. He can convert ashes and brokenness, woundedness and damage, into life that can actually be fruitful.

MG: How would you define hope?
PC: I think it's being able to breathe deep—to take a full breath and relinquish your right to understand everything—to know that in taking the next step there will be someone there for you.

MG: You know, Patsy, it was so interesting about your brother and your father and how you prayed for them so long and hoped for so long that they would come to Christ. It was really late in their lives that they did. How did that feel? Was that a journey of hope? I wonder at times if it was discouraging.
PC: There were lots of times that it was discouraging. Year after year after year you believe and nothing changes and you begin to wonder *Will this ever happen, and if so when will it take place? Is anybody here in a hurry besides me?* Some wonderful things transpired in ways that I could not have imagined, and when it did happen, there was great joy. I would say to others about their own family members—of course it's easy for me to speak now that I know that mine made that decision—hang in there, keep an open vision, believe the best, and don't give up because God's design includes families. I love that.

Again and again you see him rescue one person, and then he collects the rest of the family and puts them on the ark.

MG: You talk with such strength about the way God delivered you from the power of being controlled by fear, but I never get the picture, the feeling, that you were delivered from fear. Is that right?
PC: I think that fear is a necessary ingredient in humanity. We have reason to have fear. At times it is often an appropriate emotion. But when an emotion is so exaggerated that it becomes a controlling factor of your life, it grows into a stranglehold. I'm often asked, "Can you tell me the difference between a fear and a phobia?" When you make your decisions based around a fear, it begins to turn into a phobia. It's like if a friend asks me to go to lunch and I think to myself, *If I go to lunch I'll have to make six lefthand turns, go on the freeway for three miles, and park in an area where I don't feel safe. No, I won't be able to join you for lunch.* I will have based it all on my fears. That's when they begin to become controlling phobias, the measuring sticks for your choices.

MG: What do you do now when you feel afraid?
PC: I found the most important thing is to face it. I have to step right up to it and walk right through it. That is when it loses all it's strength over me. Fear has friends...one fear is just waiting for the rest to show up. He asks, "Will you let me in?" but what he's really asking is, "Will you let *us* in? We've come together. We are legion."

MG: It's really encouraging to me in the book and in everything you say and in watching your life that you don't pretend that you're now fixed, and that's why you have something to say.
PC: The repair job on me is a longterm process. This is no easy fix here. I would imagine that as long as I'm in this earthsuit He'll still be fixing me. My grandmother lived to be ninety-seven and a half, and she was still having repairs done on her heart and mind and attitude. So there's always something else. I love the expansiveness

163

of the fact that we always have the opportunity to learn more.

MG: One of the first things I ever heard you say when I met you eight years ago was that you wanted to get fixed in the night, to go to bed, and wake up righteous.
PC: Yes, I wanted it easy, fast, and convenient with no pain. I had already hurt enough. I didn't want to hurt, and I didn't want to work hard. I didn't want to have to change, but I did want to be different. I wanted the Lord to be a cheap date, but instead he makes such a rich investment and requires a great deal of response to that.

MG: How did you learn that it was a process, and how did you get comfortable in the process?
PC: At first I thought that if I could just find the one thing I needed to do and then do it, I'd be all better. The one pill, the one program, the one meeting, the one Scripture verse—if I could find what that one thing was, then I'd be OK. But I kept finding that when I did the one thing, six others would pop up that needed to be addressed, and when I finished the six, there were ten more. I began to see that you don't just arrive; you journey as long as there is breath in your body. It's a longterm process. You begin to say to yourself, *It is not a bad thing. I couldn't have learned this all in a short time without the experience of living with each new truth for awhile so it could go down deep inside of me.* I would have lost a great deal of it. In fact I remember one time Florence Littauer—one of the most multi-gifted individuals I've ever had the pleasure of knowing—said to me, "I'd like you to sit down and write how you got out of your agoraphobia." That was a wonderful discipline for me. The first thing I realized was that God began to change my mind and I had to change the way I was thinking. He has a whole counseling guidance book in the Scriptures for changing my mind.

MG: What are you hoping for now?

164

A Conversation with Patsy Clairmont

PC: Well, for my family. We're so invested in our grandchildren, wanting the very best for their little lives, to bring them up into godly young boys. I don't think you can fully say what a grandparent feels—it's so big and wide and deep and rich and lovely. I don't know if there is enough vocabulary to describe it. Because it's generational it goes down into the marrow of your bones, so I don't know that you can draw that up into words.

MG: What's interesting is that I knew you before you became a grandmother, and it is what you hoped and dreamed it would be without one trace of disappointment.
PC: Oh, it couldn't be better than to see their sweet little faces, watch them grow, and realize this is our future. They are an extension of us and will go where we will not. I find great joy and hope in that. We don't have daily responsibilities with them, but there is still a lot of responsibility for grandparents in being able to cover their grandchildren in prayer. While I might be quick to say it's my job to spoil them, the truth of it is the grandparents have a far greater responsibility. They should not indulge a child in an unhealthy way but be part of the support system to parents to really nurture and bring them up strong.

MG: Did you have trouble narrowing down information about your family? What was your biggest challenge in really describing the lifetime of someone you loved and the relationship you had with that person?
PC: That was probably one of most difficult things of the entire book, like taking the life of my mother and reducing it down to a chapter. There is so much to say and I cannot say it all, so I tried to say the things that will most capture who she was and what she was like so the readers have a rounded view of her life. I think that was the most difficult part—to capture their essence but wish I could tell more. I really had to determine to leave out many things, because nobody wants your story as long as *War and Peace*.

MG: In the book you say that your mother has Alzheimer's. How can one find hope in that kind of situation?

PC: Hope is a hard thing to talk about when it comes to a disease like Alzheimer's—except that in Christ we have eternal hope. It was something that my mother was really looking forward to—that eternal hope, heaven, our final hope. Even with her Alzheimer's she talks about heaven every single day. I understand why it's called the long good-bye; you lose them one bit at a time until their faculties are gone, and you're left with just the earthsuit and a little bit of spirit. And so you're grateful that there is an eternal hope because you can clearly see that life has limits. Alzheimer's takes everything but their lives. My sister has been incredible with our mother. She is very tender and she sees it as her mission in life not only to love her husband and her children but to take care of our mother and to make sure she is well tended to by family. It has been a great gift to us all. I don't think that is for everybody. I could not do that for Mom with what I do. The family all supports her though; it is a real team effort.

MG: Having written many books, would this be one of the easiest or hardest?

PC: Emotionally it was one of the most difficult projects I've ever worked on. The reality check of seeing all of my flaws, my failures, all at one time was startling. Yet, it was a picture of God's grace and mercy toward me—how he was be able to draw me out of this emotional bind I was in and put me in a solid place. That he would open doors for me I never expected, that he would give me the opportunity to speak for Women of Faith all over the nation, that he would allow me the desire of my heart—to be a writer—it's just more than I can comprehend.

MG: Are you glad you wrote it?

PC: I am. I am. It was a hard, hard thing, but I'm glad I did it. Being vulnerable was sometimes a little scary. I thought about visiting an island somewhere when it first comes out—until the dust settles.

MG: What do you want to be remembered for?
PC: That I energetically and creatively loved the Lord, to the degree I am capable, and I energetically and creatively loved my family so they would see Jesus and know that I value them so very highly. Those two things I hope would be very obvious.

You know, it's really hard to answer the question of how I want to be remembered. There is a verse in the book of Acts that I've thought would make a good epitaph. It was when two of the disciples entered a town and the people saw them and they remembered that they had been with Jesus. I've always loved that and would love to be remembered for having been with Jesus.

MG: You know what I'll remember? "Look what God has done!" I think about it every weekend when you step on that stage and when you step off. I think, *Look at that! Look at her! Look what God has done!* No one would ever know the path that you have journeyed. You can't tell by looking; there is no evidence in your life today "from whence you've come." But then when you go to this extreme to open your heart and your life and say, "Look where I was, look what God has done..."
PC: I want to offer hope to people who are wondering, *What could I ever do and how can God use me? I don't have an education or I don't have enough degrees or I don't have...*whatever it is they feel they are missing. I want them to see that there is hope for us all.

MG: How has your family reacted to your writing your story?
PC: I've processed some of the chapters with family, like my sons. I wanted to make sure that they were comfortable, that I wasn't divulging anything that would dismay or embarrass them. My husband was also very generous to allow me not only to make myself vulnerable but also to use parts of his story, things that he was willing to have revealed if it would bring hope to someone else.

MG: Did you leave out anyone in telling your story that you wished were included?

PC: Absolutely. It's impossible to include everyone. I find the longer I live the more I am aware of the significant investments many have made in my life. For instance, I traveled with Florence Littauer for thirteen years, and even though I mention her, there is so much more I could share. You can't work together and live on the road with each other without having a truckload of experiences. Actually, if I wrote about those developmental years I'd probably have a twelve-volume encyclopedia.

Another example is my Women of Faith cohorts: Marilyn Meberg, Sheila Walsh, Nicole Johnson, Thelma Wells, Luci Swindoll, Barbara Johson, and you, Mary. I have been with all of you for eight years. We have laughed, cried, grieved, disagreed, and celebrated together. God continues to use you and the others to help hone me. Each has contributed to my ongoing development. When you travel together as frequently as we do (twenty-five to thirty weekends a year) you become family with all the dynamics that brings. So, it seems as though I should have told of the countless ways you all have influenced my life. . . . but perhaps that's another book or two.

Then there is the semi-load of dear friends who have made my life richer, sweeter, and deeper; Edith Gelaude (my cherished pal and mentor for over twenty-eight years), Margret Zander, RuthAnn Bell, Shirley Valade, Lana Bateman, Mary Ann Tanner, Joyce Chaplin, Eleanor Barzler, Marilyn Van Wingerden, Danya Clairmont, Barb Ott, Ann Meredith, Pat Wenger, Nancy Stephenson, Nancy Berrens, Jan Silvious, Babbie Mason, Beth Moore, Sandy Smith, Ellie Lofaro, and Kathy Troccoli.

MG: If this book, your story, were made into a movie, who would you think should play you?

PC: Bette Midler, because she's exceedingly verbal, visual, and feisty. Besides, I've always wanted to be a redhead!